Introduction to Project Finance

T0363869

Essential Capital Markets

Books in the series:

Cash Flow Forecasting
Corporate Valuation
Credit Risk Management
Finance of International Trade
Mergers and Acquisitions
Portfolio Management in Practice
Introduction to Project Finance
Syndicated Lending

Introduction to Project Finance

Edited by
Andrew Fight

AMSTERDAM • BOSTON • HEIDELBERG • LONDON • NEW YORK • OXFORD
PARIS • SAN DIEGO • SAN FRANCISCO • SINGAPORE • SYDNEY • TOKYO
Butterworth-Heinemann is an imprint of Elsevier

Butterworth-Heinemann is an imprint of Elsevier
Linacre House, Jordan Hill, Oxford OX2 8DP, UK
30 Corporate Drive, Suite 400, Burlington, MA 01803, USA

First edition 2005
Reprinted 2006

British Library Cataloguing in Publication Data
A catalogue record for this book is available from the British Library

Library of Congress Cataloging-in-Publication Data: 2005923901

ISBN–13: 978-0-7506-5905-5

For information on all Butterworth-Heinemann publications
visit our website at books.elsevier.com

Transfered to Digital Printing 2009

Contents

Preface   vii

1   Overview of project finance   1
Introduction to project finance   1
Uses for project finance   2
Why use project financing   3
Description of a typical project finance transaction   8
Parties to a project financing   11
Financing sources used in project financing   32

2   Understanding key project risks   45
Entity risks   45
Transaction risks   50
Mitigating and managing project risks   64
Security   73
Insurance issues   77

3   Evaluating the project   81
The offering memorandum   81
Legislation relating to information memoranda   83
Information memorandum issues   87
Credit risk appraisal: general considerations   108

4 Contractual framework **112**

General 112
Pre-development agreements 112
Construction agreements 113
Contractors bonds 114
Operating and maintenance agreements 115
Sponsor support agreements 116
Management agreements 116
Representations and warranties 117
Project loan/credit agreements 118
Security agreements 137

5 Project financing in the economy **139**

Project financing and the privatization agenda 139
Project finance tables 145
The UK PFI model 145

Appendices **151**

Appendix 1: Generally accepted risk principles risk map 151
Appendix 2: Credit rating agency rating scales 153
Appendix 3: Country risk criteria 156
Appendix 4: World Bank country categories 166

Glossary **175**

Suggested reading **197**

Index **199**

Preface

Welcome to this book on project finance.

This book is presented in five chapters, each of which treats a specific part of the project finance process. The individual chapters cover the following topics:

- Overview of project finance
- Understanding key project risks
- Evaluating project
- Contractual framework
- Project financing in the economy

Appendices, a glossary and a list of suggested readings complete the book.

This book aims to explain the background and raison d'être of project finance as one of the mechanisms of the capital markets to provide finance to large scale projects, the players and mechanics in project financing, and the various sources of finance available in project finance.

Since most project financings are structured with a view to syndication in the international capital markets (indeed project finance could be considered a specialized subset of the syndicated lending market), it is suggested that this book be read in conjunction with the *Syndicated*

Lending book in the series, thereby linking the structuring of the project finance facility to the marketing issues involved in a loan syndication.

Similarly, the cash flow forecasting elements of project finance are treated in the *Cash Flow Forecasting* book in this series.

We believe that this book *Introduction to Project Finance* in the Essential Capital Markets Series, will be informative and instructional, and an indispensable aid to persons seeking to understand this important area of banking.

Andrew Fight
www.andrewfight.com

Chapter 1

Overview of project finance

Introduction to project finance

What is 'project finance'? The term features prominently in the press, more specifically with respect to infrastructure, public and private venture capital needs. The press often refers to huge projects, such as building infrastructure projects like highways, Eurotunnel, metro systems, or airports. It is a technique that has been used to raise huge amounts of capital and promises to continue to do so, in both developed and developing countries, for the foreseeable future.

While project finance bears certain similarities to syndicated lending, there are a host of specific issues that mean that it is essentially a specialized discipline unto itself, effectively a discrete subset of syndicated lending.

Project finance is generally used to refer to a non-recourse or limited recourse financing structure in which debt, equity and credit enhancement are combined for the construction and operation, or the refinancing, of a particular facility in a capital-intensive industry.

Credit appraisals and debt terms are typically based on project cash flow forecasts as opposed to the creditworthiness of the sponsors and the actual value of the project assets. Forecasting is therefore at the heart of project financing techniques. Project financing, together with the equity from the project sponsors, must be enough to cover all the costs related to the development of the project as well as working capital needs.

Project finance risks are therefore highly specific and it is essential that participants such as commercial bankers, investment bankers, general contractors, subcontractors, insurance companies, suppliers and customers understand these risks since they will all be participating in an interlocking structure.

These various participants have differing contractual obligations, and the resultant risk and reward varies with the function and performance of these various parties. Ideally, the debt servicing will be supported by the project cash flow dynamics as opposed to the participants, who at best provide limited coverage.

Uses for project finance

Project finance techniques have enabled projects to be built in markets using private capital. These private finance techniques are a key element in scaling back government financing, a central pillar of the current ideological agenda whose goals are well articulated by Grover Norquist, a US Republican ideologue and lobbyist, who says 'I don't want to abolish government. I simply want to reduce it to the size where I can drag it into the bathroom and drown it in the bathtub.' On the basis of such ideological agendas and lobbyists' machinations are the macroeconomic policies, upon which project finance feeds, made, thus transferring the control of public services from the electorate to private, unaccountable and uncoordinated interests.

Such agendas make project financing a key method of using private capital to achieve private ownership of public services such as energy, transportation and other infrastructure development initiatives. The goal ultimately is to make government irrelevant and achieve a two-tier society where government panders to the marginalized and infrastructure development and exploitation are handed over to private capital, free from the encumbrances of electoral mandates. Some of these sectors include:

- **Energy**   Project finance is used to build energy infrastructure in industrialized countries as well as in emerging markets.
- **Oil**   Development of new pipelines and refineries are also successful uses of project finance. Large natural gas pipelines and oil refineries

have been financed with this model. Before the use of project finance, such facilities were financed either by the internal cash generation of oil companies, or by governments.

- **Mining**   Project finance is used to develop the exploitation of natural resources such as copper, iron ore, or gold mining operations in countries as diverse as Chile, Ghana and Australia.
- **Highways**   New roads are often financed with project finance techniques since they lend themselves to the cash flow based model of repayment.
- **Telecommunications**   The burgeoning demand for telecommunications and data transfer via the Internet in developed and developing countries necessitates the use of project finance techniques to fund this infrastructure development.
- **Other**   Other sectors targeted for a private takeover of public utilities and services via project finance mechanisms include pulp and paper projects, chemical facilities, manufacturing, hospitals, retirement care facilities, prisons, schools, airports and ocean-going vessels.

Why use project financing

Non-recourse/limited recourse

Non-recourse/limited recourse is one of the key distinguishing factors underlying project finance. Classic long term lending typically depends on cash flows but the facilities' ultimate credit rationale resides upon the creditworthiness of the borrower, since the lender will have a claim over the company's assets.

In a project financing, this is rarely the case since the size of the operation may dwarf the size of the participating companies' balance sheets. Moreover, the borrowing entity may be a special purpose vehicle with no credit history.

This is why it is useful to distinguish between non-recourse and limited recourse project financings.

- **Non-recourse project financing**   Non-recourse project financing means that there is no recourse to the project sponsor's assets for the debts or liabilities of an individual project. Non-recourse financing therefore depends purely on the merits of a project rather than the credit-worthiness of the project sponsor. Credit appraisal therefore resides on the anticipated cash flows of the project, and is independent of the creditworthiness of the project sponsors. In such a scenario, the project sponsor has no direct legal obligation to repay the project debt or make interest payments.

■ **Limited recourse project finance**   In most project financings, there are limited obligations and responsibilities of the project sponsor; that is, the financing is limited recourse. Security, for example, may not suffice to fully guarantee a project. The main issue here is not that the guarantees offered fully mitigate the project but rather implicate the sponsor's involvement sufficiently deeply in order to fully incentivize the sponsor to ensure the technical success of the project.

How much recourse is necessary to support a financing is determined based on the unique characteristics of the project. The project risks and the extent of support forthcoming from the sponsors will directly impact the risk profile of the project, as well as the syndication strategy.

For example, if the lenders perceive that a substantial risk exists during the construction phase of a project, they could require that the project sponsor inject additional equity should certain financial ratio covenants be violated. Other mechanisms subject to negotiations between the agent bank and project sponsors are also possible.

Advantages of project finance

■ **Non-recourse/limited recourse financing**   Non-recourse project finan-cing does not impose any obligation to guarantee the repayment of the project debt on the project sponsor. This is important because capital adequacy requirements and credit ratings mean that assuming finan-cial commitments to a large project may adversely impact the com-pany's financial structure and credit rating (and ability to access funds in the capital markets).

■ **Off balance sheet debt treatment**   The main reason for choosing project finance is to isolate the risk of the project, taking it off balance sheet so that project failure does not damage the owner's financial condition. This may be motivated by genuine economic arguments such as maintaining existing financial ratios and credit ratings. Theoretically, therefore, the project sponsor may retain some real financial risk in the project as a motivating factor, however, the off balance sheet treatment *per se* will effectively not affect the company's investment rating by credit rating analysts.

- **Leveraged debt**   Debt is advantageous for project finance sponsors in that share issues (and equity dilution) can be avoided. Furthermore, equity requirements for projects in developing countries are influenced by many factors, including the country, the project economics, whether any other project participants invest equity in the project, and the eagerness for banks to win the project finance business.
- **Avoidance of restrictive covenants in other transactions**   Because the project financed is separate and distinct from other operations and projects of the sponsor, existing restrictive covenants do not typically apply to the project financing. A project finance structure permits a project sponsor to avoid restrictive covenants, such as debt coverage ratios and provisions that cross-default for a failure to pay debt, in the existing loan agreements and indentures at the project sponsor level.
- **Favourable tax treatment**   Project finance is often driven by tax-efficient considerations. Tax allowances and tax breaks for capital investments etc. can stimulate the adoption of project finance. Projects that contract to provide a service to a state entity can use these tax breaks (or subsidies) to inflate the profitability of such ventures.
- **Favourable financing terms**   Project financing structures can enhance the credit risk profile and therefore obtain more favourable pricing than that obtained purely from the project sponsor's credit risk profile.
- **Political risk diversification**   Establishing SPVs (special purpose vehicles) for projects in specific countries quarantines the project risks and shields the sponsor (or the sponsor's other projects) from adverse developments.
- **Risk sharing**   Allocating risks in a project finance structure enables the sponsor to spread risks over all the project participants, including the lender. The diffusion of risk can improve the possibility of project

success since each project participant accepts certain risks; however, the multiplicity of participating entities can result in increased costs which must be borne by the sponsor and passed on to the end consumer – often consumers that would be better served by public services.

- **Collateral limited to project assets**   Non-recourse project finance loans are based on the premise that collateral comes only from the project assets. While this is generally the case, limited recourse to the assets of the project sponsor is sometimes required as a way of incentivizing the sponsor.
- **Lenders are more likely to participate in a workout than foreclose** The non-recourse or limited recourse nature of project finance means that collateral (a half-completed factory) has limited value in a liquidation scenario. Therefore, if the project is experiencing difficulties, the best chance of success lies in finding a workout solution rather than foreclosing. Lenders will therefore more likely cooperate in a workout scenario to minimize losses.

Disadvantages of project finance

- **Complexity of risk allocation**   Project financings are complex transactions involving many participants with diverse interests. This results in conflicts of interest on risk allocation amongst the participants and protracted negotiations and increased costs to compensate third parties for accepting risks.
- **Increased lender risk**   Since banks are not equity risk takers, the means available to enhance the credit risk to acceptable levels are limited, which results in higher prices. This also necessitates expensive processes of due diligence conducted by lawyers, engineers and other specialized consultants.
- **Higher interest rates and fees**   Interest rates on project financings may be higher than on direct loans made to the project sponsor since the transaction structure is complex and the loan documentation lengthy. Project finance is generally more expensive than classic lending because of:
  - the time spent by lenders, technical experts and lawyers to evaluate the project and draft complex loan documentation;
  - the increased insurance cover, particularly political risk cover;

- the costs of hiring technical experts to monitor the progress of the project and compliance with loan covenant;
- the charges made by the lenders and other parties for assuming additional risks.

- **Lender supervision** In order to protect themselves, lenders will want to closely supervise the management and operations of the project (whilst at the same time avoiding any liability associated with excessive interference in the project). This supervision includes site visits by lender's engineers and consultants, construction reviews, and monitoring construction progress and technical performance, as well as financial covenants to ensure funds are not diverted from the project. This lender supervision is to ensure that the project proceeds as planned, since the main value of the project is cash flow via successful operation.

- **Lender reporting requirements** Lenders will require that the project company provides a steady stream of financial and technical information to enable them to monitor the project's progress. Such reporting includes financial statements, interim statements, reports on technical progress, delays and the corrective measures adopted, and various notices such as events of default.

- **Increased insurance coverage** The non-recourse nature of project finance means that risks need to be mitigated. Some of this risk can be mitigated via insurance available at commercially acceptable rates. This however can greatly increase costs, which in itself, raises other risk issues such as pricing and successful syndication.

- **Transaction costs may outweigh the benefits** The complexity of the project financing arrangement can result in a transaction whose costs are so great as to offset the advantages of the project financing structure. The time-consuming nature of negotiations amongst various parties and government bodies, restrictive covenants, and limited control of project assets, and burgeoning legal costs may all work together to render the transaction unfeasible.

Common misconceptions about project finance

There are several misconceptions about project finance:

- The assumption that lenders should in all circumstances look to the project as the exclusive source of debt service and repayment is excessively rigid and can create difficulties when negotiating between the project participants.

■ Lenders do not require a high level of equity from the project sponsors. This may be true in absolute terms but should not obscure the fact that an equity participation is an effective measure to ensure that the project sponsors are incentivized for success.

■ The assets of the project provide 100% security. Whilst lenders normally look for primary and secondary sources of repayment (cash flow plus security on project assets), the realizable value of such assets (e.g. roads, tunnels and pipelines which cannot be moved) are such that the security is next to meaningless when compared against future anticipated cash flows. Security therefore is primarily taken in order to ensure that participants are committed to the project rather than the intention of providing a realistic method of ensuring repayment.

■ The project's technical and economic performance will be measured according to pre-set tests and targets. Lenders will seek flexibility in interpreting the results of such negotiations in order to protect their positions. Borrowers on the other hand will argue for purely objective tests in order to avoid being subjected to subjective value judgements on the part of the lenders.

■ Lenders will not want to abandon the project as long as some surplus cash flow is being generated over operating costs, even if this level represents an uneconomic return to the project sponsors.

■ Lenders will often seek assurances from the host government about the risks of expropriation and availability of foreign exchange. Often these risks are covered by insurance or export credit guarantee support. The involvement of a multilateral organization such as the World Bank or regional development banks in a project tends to 'validate' a project and reassure lenders' concerns about political risk.

Description of a typical project finance transaction

Project finance transactions are complex transactions that often require numerous players in interdependent relationships. To illustrate, we provide

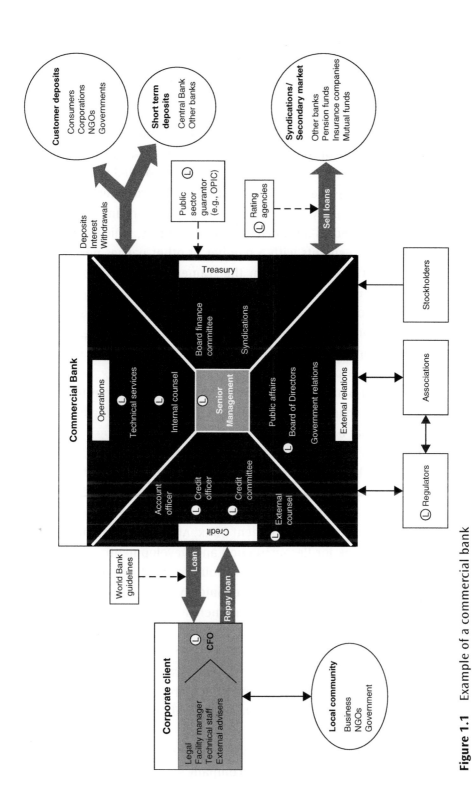

Figure 1.1 Example of a commercial bank

an organization diagram of the various players seen from the viewpoint of an agent bank in a generic project finance transaction:

■ The core of a project financing is typically the project company, which is a special purpose vehicle (SPV) that consists of the consortium share-holders (such as contractors or operators who may be investors or have other interests in the project). The SPV is formed specifically to build and operate the project. The SPV can be structured either as a local project company or a joint venture (JV) consortium.
■ The SPV is created as an independent legal entity, which enters into contractual agreements with a number of other parties necessary to the project. The contracts form the framework for project viability and control the allocation of risks.
■ The project company enters into negotiations with the host govern-ment to obtain all requisite permits and authorizations, e.g. an oil or gas production licence, a mining concession, or a permit to build and operate a power plant.
■ A syndicate of banks may enter into a financial agreement to finance the project company. There may be several classes of lending banks, e.g.
 ■ international banks lending foreign currency;
 ■ local banks lending domestic currency for local costs;
 ■ export credit agencies lending or guaranteeing credits to finance suppliers to the project of their national equipment; and
 ■ international agencies lending or guaranteeing development credits (World Bank, Asian Development Bank, African Development Bank, European Bank for Reconstruction and Development).
■ The project company enters into various contracts necessary to con-struct and operate the project: The major types of contracts include:
 ■ EPC contract (engineering, procurement and construction) – to build and construct the project facility;
 ■ O&M contract (operation and management) – to manage and oper-ate the facility and project during its operational phase;
 ■ supply contract (the project company enters into contracts with sup-pliers to ensure an uninterrupted supply of raw materials necessary for the project);
 ■ off-take agreements (the project company enters into contracts with purchasers of the project company's product or service).

Project phases

Project financings can be divided into two distinct stages:

- Construction and development phase – here, the loan will be extended and debt service may be postponed, either by rolling-up interest or by allowing further drawdowns to finance interest payments prior to the operation phase. The construction phase is the period of highest risk for lenders since resources are being committed and construction must be completed before cash flow can be generated. Margins might be higher than during other phases of the project to compensate for the higher risks. The risks will be mitigated by taking security over the construction contract and related performance bonds.
- Operation phase – here, the lenders will have further security since the project will begin to generate cash flows. Debt service will normally be tailored to the actual cash flows generated by the project – typically a 'dedicated percentage' of net cash flows will, via security structures such as blocked accounts, go to the lenders automatically with the remainder transferred to the project company. The terms of the loan will frequently provide for alternative arrangements should cash flows generate an excess or shortfall due to unanticipated economic or political risks arising.

Parties to a project financing

As we saw in the previous section, there are several parties in a project financing. Here is a list, albeit non-exhaustive, of the most usual ones.

Project company

The project company is the legal entity that will own, develop, construct, operate and maintain the project. The project company is generally an SPV created in the project host country and therefore subject to the laws of that country (unless appropriate 'commissions' can be paid so that key government officials can grant 'exceptions' to the project). The SPV will be controlled by its equity owners. The control mechanism may be defined in a charter, a joint venture agreement or partnership agreement and may also be subject to local laws. Its only activity will be to own and operate the project.

Sponsor

The project sponsor is the entity that manages the project. The sponsor generally becomes equity owner of the SPV and will receive any profit either via equity ownership (dividend streams) or management contracts (fees). The project sponsor generally brings management, operational, and technical experience to the project. The project sponsor may be required to provide guarantees to cover certain liabilities or risks of the project. This is not so much for security purposes but rather to ensure that the sponsor is appropriately incentivized as to the project's success.

Borrower

The borrowing entity might or might not be the SPV. This depends on the structure of the financing and of the operation of the project (which will themselves be determined by a host of factors such as tax, exchange controls, the availability of security and the enforceability of claims in the host country). A project may in fact have several 'borrowers', for example, the construction company, the operating company, suppliers of raw materials to the project and purchasers (off-takers) of the project's production.

Financial adviser

The project sponsor may retain the services of a commercial or merchant bank to provide financial advisory services to the sponsor. The financial adviser theoretically will be familiar with the project host country and be able to advise on local legal requirements and transaction structures to ensure that the loan documentation and financial structure are properly assembled.

A financial consultant can also advise on how to arrange the financing of the project, taking into consideration streaming cash flows, creation of shell offshore companies, tax avoidance, currency speculation, desirable locales for the project and capital required. Consultants can add the imprimatur of legality to the creation of such convoluted structures and provide help with accounting issues relating to the above other issues, such as the expected cost of the project, interest rates, inflation rates, the projected economics of operations and the anticipated cash flow.

The financial adviser finally can assist in the preparation of the information memorandum regarding the proposed project. As the name suggests, the information memorandum provides information on the project, and is presented in glowing positive terms as an inducement for banks to participate in the financing, and achieve a successful syndication (despite disclaimers stating to the contrary that the memorandum is not a recommendation to participate in the facility and no responsibility can be taken for the accuracy of the information provided therein).

The lenders

The large size of projects being financed often requires the syndication of the financing. For example, the Eurotunnel project financing involved some 220 banks. The syndicated loan, which is treated in a separate book in this series, exists because often any one lender individually does not have the balance sheet availability due to capitalization requirements to provide the entire project loan. Other reasons may be that it wishes to limit its risk exposure in the financing or diversify its lending portfolio and avoid risk concentration.

The solution is to arrange a loan where there are several lenders forwarding funds under a single loan agreement. Such a group of lenders is often called a *syndicate*. A syndicate of banks might be chosen from as wide a range of countries as possible to discourage the host government from taking action to expropriate or otherwise interfere with the project and thus jeopardize its economic relations with those countries. The syndicate can also include banks from the host country, especially when there are restrictions on foreign banks taking security in the country. There are various categories of lenders in a loan syndication, typically:

- **The arranger**   The bank that arranges the syndication is called the arranging bank or lead manager. The bank typically negotiates the term sheet with the borrower as well as the credit and security documentation.

■ **The managers** The managing bank is typically a title meant to distinguish the bank from mere participants. In other words, the bank may take a large portion of the loan and syndicate it, thus assuming some of the underwriting risk. Managers can therefore broaden the geographic scope of the syndication. This role is reflected in the title which then features in the facility tombstones and any other publicity relating to the facility.

■ **The facility agent** exists to administer the administrative details of the loan on behalf of the syndicate. The facility agent is not responsible for the credit decisions of the lenders in entering into the transaction. The agent bank is responsible for mechanistic aspects of the loan such as coordinating drawdowns, repayments, and communications between the parties to the finance documentation, such as serving notices and disseminating information. The Facility Agent also monitors covenant compliance and, when necessary, polls the bank group members in situations where a vote is needed (such as whether to declare a default or perfect security arrangements) and communicates these decisions to the borrower.

■ **Technical/engineering bank** as the name implies monitors the technical progress and performance of the project and liaise with the project engineers and independent experts. As such, the bank is responsible for identifying technical (engineering) events of default.

■ **Account bank** The account bank is the bank through which all project cash flows pass and are monitored, collected, and disbursed.

■ **Insurance bank** The insurance bank undertakes negotiations in connection with project insurances, to ensure that the lender's position is fully covered in terms of project insurance.

■ **The security trustee** exists where there are different groups of lenders or other creditors interested in the security and the coordination of their interests will call for the appointment of an independent trust company as security trustee.

The interrelationships of participating banks in a bank syndicate often appears post-syndication in a 'tombstone', which is a form of advertising for the successful syndicating bank.

Technical adviser

Technical experts advise the project sponsor and lenders on technical matters about which the sponsor and lenders have limited knowledge (oil, mining, fuel, environmental). Such experts typically prepare reports, such as feasibility reports, for the project sponsor and lenders, and may monitor the progress of the project, possibly acting as the arbiter in the event of disagreements between the sponsors and the lenders over the satisfaction of the performance covenants and tests stipulated in the finance documents.

Lawyers

The international nature and complexity of project financing necessitates the retention of experienced international law firms. Project finance lawyers provide legal experience with specific experience of project finance structures, experience with the underlying industry and knowledge of project contracts, debt and equity documents, credit enhancement and international transactions.

Project finance lawyers provide advice on all aspects of a project, including laws and regulations; permits; organization of project entities; negotiating and drafting of project construction, operation, sale and supply contracts; negotiating and drafting of debt and equity documents; bankruptcy; tax; and similar matters.

It is advisable to involve the lawyers at an early stage to ensure that the structure of the financing is properly conceived from the outset and is tax-efficient. Local lawyers in the host country of the project are also necessary in opining on various local legal matters in connection with the project financing. They are particularly useful with respect to assessing the enforceability of claims on project assets located in the host country.

Equity investors

These may be lenders or project sponsors who do not expect to have an active management role as the project goes on stream. In the case of

BANQUE PSA FINANCE HOLDING

and

PEUGEOT FINANCE INTERNATIONAL N.V.
FRF 12,500,000,000
Multicurrency Revolving Loan Facility
Incorporating a FRF4, 190,000,000 Swingline Facility

guaranteed by
BANQUE PSA FINANCE HOLDING

Arrangers

ABN-Amro Bank NV	Credit Suisse/CS First Boston Limited
NatWest Markets	Société Générale

Senior lead managers

Banque Indosuez	Banque National de Paris
Banque Paribas	Commerzbank Aktiengesellschaft, Succursale de Paris
Crédit Lyonnais	Deutsche Bank AG, Succursale de Paris
Dresdner Bank Luxembourg SA	Midland Bank Plc, Paris Branch
Morgan Guaranty Trust Company of New York	Union Bank of Switzerland

Lead managers

Argentaria/Banco Extérior de España, Paris Branch	Banque Fédérative du Crédit Mutuel
Banque Française du Commerce Extérieur	Bayerische Vereinsbank AG, Succursale de Paris
Caisse Centrale des Banques Populaires	Caisse des Dépôts et Consignations
Crédit Commercial de France	Crédit Industriel et Commercial de Paris
Den Danske Bank	DG Bank, Deutsche Genossenschaftsbank
The Fuji Bank Limited	ING Bank, Paris Branch
Rabobank, Succursale de Paris	Enskilda
The Sumitomo Bank Limited, Paris Branch	The Toronto-Dominion Bank
Unicrédit/Crédit Agricole Group	WestLB Group

Managers

Banca Commerciale Italiana SpA, London Branch	Banca Monte dei Paschi di Siena SpA, London Branch
Banca Nazionale del Lavoro SpA, Succursale de Paris	Banca Popolare di Milano, London Branch
Banco Bilbao Vizcaya SA, Paris Branch	Banco Santander SA, Paris Branch
Bank of America NT & SA	The Bank of Tokyo Ltd, Paris Branch
Banque Bruxelles Lambert France SA	Banque Sanpaolo
Banque Worms	BHF-Bank Aktiengesellschaft
Caja de Madrid	The Chase Manhattan Bank NA
Crédit du Nord	Credito Italiano SpA, Paris Branch
The Dai-Ichi Kangyo Bank Limited, Paris Branch	Generale Bank
Kredietbank, Succursale Française	Lyonnaise de Banque
The Mitsubishi Bank Limited, Succursale de Paris	NationsBank
Royal Bank of Canada Group	Republic National Bank of New York
The Royal Bank of Scotland plc	The Sanwa Bank, Paris Branch
Scotiabank (Ireland) Limited	Sogenal, Strasbourg
Standard Chartered Bank	

Facility and swingline agent
ABN-Amro Bank NV

Figure 1.2

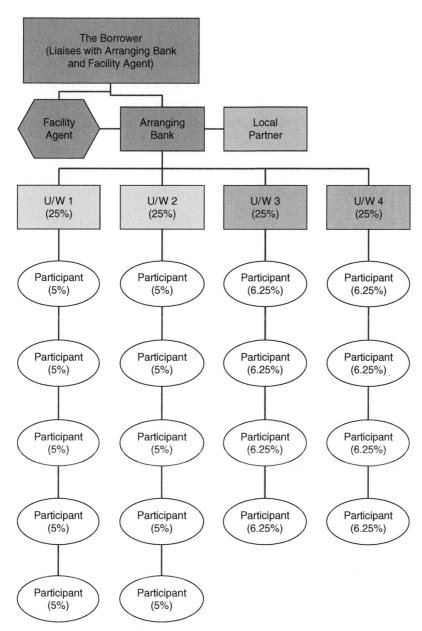

Figure 1.3   Hypothetical loan syndication breakdown

lenders, they are putting equity alongside their debt as a way to obtain an enhanced return if the project is successful. In most cases, the equity investment is combined with agreements that allow the equity investor to sell its equity to the project owner if the equity investor wishes to get out. Third party investors normally look to invest in a project on a much longer time scale than a contractor who in most cases will want to sell out once the construction has reached completion. Many third party investors are development or equity funds, which diversify their portfolios by investing in a number of projects. They may seek to manage the project by appointing members of their own organizations to the board of the project company.

Construction company

Since most project financings are infrastructural, the contractor is typically one of the key players in the construction period. Construction can be either of the EPC or 'turnkey' variety. EPC, or engineer, procure, and construct, is when the construction company builds the facility as per an already designated specifications. Turnkey, on the other hand, is when the contractor designs, engineers, procures and constructs the facility, assuming all responsibility for on-time completion. In both cases, it is important that the construction company selected has a track record of successful project management and completion. In many large projects, consortia of constructors may become involved either for sheer economies of scale or for political reasons. In such cases, lenders prefer members of the consortia to undertake joint and several liability since the risk of failure of performance is the total responsibility of each member of the consortium.

Most projects are structured on the basis that only one turnkey or EPC contractor will be employed. The various designers, contractors and subcontractors participating in the project will therefore be under the overall control of the project manager. This enables the coordination and streamlining of reporting lines.

Regulatory agencies

Projects naturally are subject to local laws and regulations. These may include environmental, zoning, permits and taxes. Publicly owned projects also will be subject to various procurement and public contract laws. It is important to ensure that a project has received all the requisite permissions and licences before committing financial resources. In many markets, such 'roadblocks' may require extensive and time-consuming preparation for applying for the requisite government permission followed by indeterminate waiting. Another possibility is the lobbying of local political figures or the payment of large 'commissions' to persons in the host country's government which may or may not have the clout to obtain the requisite approval. For example, a Mercedes 600 SLC given to an individual in the host country's government may accelerate the requisite permission for an oil rig to enter or leave the state's territorial waters. Then again, it may not. Therefore, 'caveat emptor' or in this case, 'know your prince'.

Export credit agencies

Export credit agencies (ECAs) promote trade or other interests of an organizing country. They are generally nationalistic in purpose and nationalistic and political in operation. Funding of bilateral agencies generally comes from their organizing governments. Government-supported export financing includes pre-export working capital, short term export receivables financing and long term financing.

ECAs play important roles in infrastructure and other projects in emerging markets by stimulating international trade. They normally provide low cost financing arrangements to local manufacturers who wish to transport their technology to foreign lands.

ECAs also provide political risk insurance to projects. This has an effect of 'validating' the project as lenders believe that foreign governments are reluctant to curry disfavour by defaulting on facilities granted by a foreign bilateral agency.

United States Export–Import Bank

The Export–Import Bank of the United States (Ex–Im Bank) is the official export credit agency of the United States. Ex–Im Bank's mission is to assist in financing the export of US goods and services to international markets.

Ex–Im Bank enables US companies – large and small – to turn export opportunities into real sales that help to maintain and create US jobs and contribute to a stronger national economy.

Ex–Im Bank does not compete with private sector lenders but provides export financing products that fill gaps in trade financing. It assumes credit and country risks that the private sector is unable or unwilling to accept. It also helps to level the playing field for US exporters by matching the financing that other governments provide to their exporters.

Ex–Im Bank provides working capital guarantees (pre-export financing), export credit insurance (post-export financing) and loan guarantees and direct loans (buyer financing). No transaction is too large or too small. On average, 85% of its transactions directly benefit US small businesses.

Ministry of Economy Trade and Industry (Japan)

The Export–Import Insurance Division of Japan's Ministry of Economy Trade and Industry ('METI', ex MITI) is an agency of the Government of Japan. It provides insurance coverage to Japanese companies and non-Japanese companies registered in Japan. MITI coverage can be combined with OPIC coverage to cover the entire bank group, depending upon the location of members of the bank group. There is no maximum amount of coverage.

Export–Import Bank of Japan

The Export–Import Bank of Japan provides limited political risk coverage Eligibility is limited to loans from financial institutions in Japan (including branches of foreign banks), for funding recently privatized businesses and regulated industries in developing countries. Significant is that the coverage is not limited to Japanese export financing. The maximum coverage is generally 95% for a maximum term of 12 years.

Export Credits Guarantee Department

ECGD, the Export Credits Guarantee Department, is the UK's official export credit agency. It works closely with exporters, project sponsors, banks and buyers to help UK exporters of capital equipment and project-related goods and services to win business and invest overseas.

ECGD was originally set up in 1919 to help British exporters re-establish their trading positions following the disruption caused by the Great War.

This assistance largely took the form of providing insurance against the commercial and political risks of not being paid by overseas buyers after goods were exported. In 1991, the arm of ECGD which dealt with exporters who traded on short terms of credit (i.e. up to two years) was sold to NCM Credit Insurance Ltd. Exporters of this type of goods, e.g. consumable items, can now obtain credit insurance from a number of companies in the private market. ECGD still provides exporters of British capital goods and services with finance and insurance packages to help them win valuable overseas orders. It also insures British companies who invest abroad against the political risks of a non-return on their investments.

ECGD is a separate Department of the British Government, reporting to the Secretary of State for Trade and Industry. It derives its powers from the 1991 Export and Investment Guarantees Act.

ECGD operates on a break-even basis, charging exporters premium at levels to match the risk on non-payment. From this, reserves are built up to pay for claims if overseas buyers/borrowers default on payments. ECGD would then seek to make recovery of claims paid through negotiation with overseas buyers/borrowers.

Compagnie Française d'Assurances Commerciale Exterieure

Founded in 1946, Coface is a subsidiary of Natexis Banques Populaires and the Banque Populaire Group, whose regulatory capital (tier 1) amounted to €12.2 billion at 31 December 2003. Coface facilitates global trade by offering companies solutions to manage, finance and protect their customer portfolio and enabling them to outsource all or part of their receivables management, as well as the related risks.

Coface has over 4000 employees serving 85 000 clients, with an organization in each country based on integrated sales forces and four product lines: credit insurance; credit information and corporate ratings; receivables management; and factoring and receivables securitization. Coface also offers three other business lines: guarantee insurance, receivables management training and, in France, public procedures management for export guarantees on behalf of the State.

Coface has subsidiaries or branches in 57 countries and offers local services in 91 countries through its partners in the CreditAlliance network, united by shared credit risk management systems (the Common Risk System).

Export Development Corporation of Canada

The Export Development Corporation of Canada (EDC) provides political risk coverage to projects located in eligible countries. The product or service exported generally must be at least 50% in Canadian content. The maximum coverage is CN$ 100 million. The maximum term is 15 years.

Other OCED government insurance entities

Each member country of the Organization for Economic Co-operation and Development (OECD) has established political risk insurance programs similar to the United States OPIC program.

Current members are Australia, Austria, Belgium, Canada, Denmark, Finland, France, Germany, Greece, Iceland, Ireland, Italy, Japan, Luxembourg, the Netherlands, New Zealand, Norway, Portugal, Spain, Sweden, Switzerland, Turkey, the United Kingdom, the United States and its territories. Some of these are summarized in Table 1.1.

Commercial insurance

Complementary and alternative political risk insurance is offered by a small community of insurers. These include:

- Lloyd's of London
- American International Underwriters
- Unistat Assurance
- Citicorp International Trade Indemnity, Inc.

In general, these coverages are of a limited term of one to three years, and do not typically match the term of the project debt. However, private insurance companies are generally more flexible than OPIC, MIGA or the export–import agencies because they are not constrained by public policy considerations. In addition, they provide benefits of confidentiality and possible cost savings associated with negotiation of complete, single source insurance protection for a project, including casualty, liability

Table 1.1   Major ECAs operating today (listed by country)

Australia	**Export Finance and Insurance Corporation** (EFIC) provides export financing and commercial and political risk insurance
Austria	**Oesterreichische Kontrollbank AG**
Belgium	**Office National du Decroire** (OND) provides export credit insurance as the credit enhancement for commercial bank loans
Canada	**Export Development Corporation** (**EDC**) provides export financing and insurance support
Denmark	**Eksportkreditraadet** – the Danish export finance organization. It provides only guarantees.
Finland	**Finish Export Credit Limited** – a joint stock company, majority owned by the government. It provides financing to exporters, buyers and bank to bank credit
France	**Compagnie Française d'Assurance pour le Commerce Exterieur** provides commercial and political risk insurance
Germany	**Kreditanstalt fiir Wiederaufbau** provides export credits. Also, Hermes Kreditvers cherungs AG, a private company, provides credit premium of risk insurance, and Ausfuhrkredit Gesellschaft, a private consortium of commercial banks, provides export credits
Italy	**Instituto Centrale per il Credito a Medio Termine** administers Italy's export credit programme. Export credit commercial and political risk insurance is provided by Sezione Speciale per Assicurazione del Credito al'Esportazione (SACE).
Japan	**Export Import Bank of Japan** provides credits to purchasing foreign entities for financing Japanese goods and services
Korea	**Export Import Bank of Korea** provides bilateral loans
Netherlands	In the Netherlands, export financing is provided by commercial banks. The Nederlandsche Credietverzekering Maatschapij provides insurance against credit risks
Norway	**Garanti instituttet for Eksportkreditt** provides loan guarantees to support export financings. Also, the Norwegian Agency for Development Cooperation, together with Eksportfinans, provides export credit. Eksportfinans is an export credit agency owned by commercial banks and GEIK

(*continued*)

Table 1.1 *(continued)*

Sweden	**Swedish International Development Authority** provides export guarantees which emanate from the Swedish Export Credits Guarantee Board
Spain	**Export Credit Insurance Company** provides commercial and political risk insurance for export credits. Concessional export credits are provided by the Institute for External Trade
UK	**Export Credit Guarantee Department** (ECGD) guarantees payment to a UK financial institution to support UK goods and services, guaranteeing exporters against payment risks resulting from commercial and political risks
USA	**Export Import Bank** operates as an independent US agency
USA	**Overseas Private Investment Corporation** (OPIC) is an agency of the United States government
Other bilateral support	Bilateral agencies also provide other support to exporting entities and their lenders, particularly for projects in developing countries. Most common is insurance against export commercial and political risks. Guarantees are also available to protect against these risks

and other insurance. On the other hand, commercial insurers rarely offer currency transfer and political violence coverage in developing countries and emerging economies.

Multilateral agencies/development banks

European Bank for Reconstruction and Development (EBRD)

The European Bank for Reconstruction and Development was established in 1991 when communism was crumbling in Central and Eastern Europe and ex-soviet countries needed support to nurture a new private sector in a democratic environment. Today the EBRD uses the tools of investment to help build market economies and democracies in 27 countries from Central Europe to Central Asia.

The EBRD is the largest single investor in the region and mobilizes significant foreign direct investment beyond its own financing. It is owned by 60 countries and two intergovernmental institutions. But despite its public sector shareholders, it invests mainly in private enterprises, usually together with commercial partners.

It provides project financing for banks, industries and businesses, both new ventures and investments in existing companies. It also works with publicly owned companies, to support privatization, restructuring state-owned firms and improvement of municipal services. The Bank uses its close relationship with governments in the region to promote policies that will bolster the business environment.

The mandate of the EBRD stipulates that it must only work in countries that are committed to democratic principles. Respect for the environment is part of the strong corporate governance attached to all EBRD investments.

Every EBRD investment must:

■ help move a country closer to a full market economy: the transition impact;
■ take risk that supports private investors and does not crowd them out;
■ apply sound banking principles.

Through its investments, the EBRD promotes:

■ structural and sectoral reforms;
■ competition, privatization and entrepreneurship;
■ stronger financial institutions and legal systems;
■ infrastructure development needed to support the private sector;
■ adoption of strong corporate governance, including environmental sensitivity; and it provides technical assistance.

World Bank

The International Bank for Reconstruction and Development (IBRD), better known as the World Bank, came into existence on 27 December 1945 following international ratification of the agreements reached at the Bretton Woods Conference.

The World Bank was originally operated as a vehicle for member countries to loan money to member countries needing foreign capital. It was structured as a financing intermediary for those countries that lacked the creditworthiness to borrow at attractive rates on their own.

The main objectives of the bank are:

- to assist in the development of member countries by facilitating the investment of capital for productive purposes;
- to promote private foreign investment by means of guarantees or participation in loans and other investments made by private investors;
- to promote the long-range balanced growth of international trade and the maintenance of equilibrium in balance of payments.

Most recently, the World Bank has assumed an ideological dimension by undertaking measures to reduce the prominence of the public sector role and increase that of the private sector. Thus, various factors must be addressed to determine whether a project will be attractive to the World Bank for participation by it. These include improvement of the business environment in accordance with the World Bank's *weltanschauungen*. Its recent track record confirms that this policy objective has taken a front seat to its original objectives of 'reducing poverty and encouraging economic development'.

Though repeatedly relied upon by impoverished governments around the world as a contributor of development finance, the Bank has been criticized by opponents of corporate 'neo-colonial' globalization for undermining the national sovereignty of recipient countries through its pursuit of economic liberalization.

One of the issues arising on repayment policy is that some loans were provided to dictators and military juntas even though the dictators did not have a popular mandate to represent the people, and following the departure or overthrow of the dictators, the hapless inhabitants of the country are then called upon to honour the loans of the despots which tyrannized them. This has the hallmarks of debts being transmitted from generation to generation, a form of slavery. A similar argument could be applied to bilateral loans made in these periods too.

Finally multilateral agencies can threaten governments with various measures should they fail to implement desired policies. The resulting dislocations and hardships borne by the indigenous population re. labour markets and cost of living variations are effectively irrelevant.

International Finance Corporation

The International Finance Corporation (IFC) promotes private sector investment in developing countries. IFC is a member of the World Bank Group and is headquartered in Washington, DC. It shares the primary objective of all World Bank Group institutions: to improve the quality of the lives of people in its developing member countries. Established in 1956, IFC is the largest multilateral source of loan and equity financing for private sector projects in the developing world. It promotes sustainable private sector development primarily by:

- financing private sector projects located in the developing world;
- helping private companies in the developing world mobilize financing in international financial markets;
- providing advice and technical assistance to businesses and governments.

IFC has 176 member countries , which collectively determine its policies and approve investments. To join IFC, a country must first be a member of the IBRD. IFC's corporate powers are vested in its Board of Governors, to which member countries appoint representatives. IFC's share capital, which is paid in, is provided by its member countries, and voting is in proportion to the number of shares held. IFC's authorized capital is $2.45 billion.

Multilateral Investment Guarantee Agency

The Multilateral Investment Guarantee Agency (MIGA) was created in 1988 as a member of the World Bank Group to promote foreign direct investment into emerging economies to improve people's lives and reduce poverty. MIGA fulfils this mandate and contributes to development by offering political risk insurance (guarantees) to investors and lenders, and by helping developing countries attract and retain private investment.

MIGA is led in its mission by four guiding principles: focusing on clients – serving investors, lenders, and host country governments by supporting private enterprise and promoting foreign investment; engaging in partnerships – working with other insurers, government agencies and international organizations to ensure complementarity of services and approach; promoting developmental impact – striving to improve the lives of people in emerging economies, consistent with the goals of host countries and sound business, environmental, and social principles; ensuring financial soundness – balancing developmental goals and financial objectives through prudent underwriting and sound risk management.

MIGA membership, which currently stands at 163, is open to all World Bank members. The agency began operations in 1988 with a capital base of $1 billion. In 1999, the MIGA Council of Governors approved a resolution for a capital increase of $850 million. Members have since contributed $655 million (or 77%) of this amount; when further pledges are converted, this should rise to $824 million, or 97%. In addition, the agency received a $150 million contribution to its recapitalization from the World Bank.

Regional development banks

Regional development banks are organized with goals similar to the World Bank, such as poverty reduction and promotion of economic growth. Rather than a global focus, however, these banks instead focus on a particular geographic region. They are owned and funded by the governments of the region and industrialized nations. These include:

- **African Development Bank** The African Development Bank (AfDB), which began operations in 1963, is a major source of public financing in Africa. The member countries include 51 African states and 25 other countries, most of which are industrialized nations.
- **Arab Fund for Economic and Social Development** Established in 1972, the Arab Fund for Economic and Social Development assists development in the member countries of the Arab League. The fund assists in financing of development projects.
- **Asian Development Bank** The Asian Development Bank is a multilateral development finance institution that engages in mostly public sector lending for development purposes in its developing member

countries in Asia and the Pacific. It pursues this goal by providing loans and technical assistance for a broad range of development activities. ADB raises funds through bond issues on the world's capital markets but also relies on members' contributions. The ADB was established in 1966 and has its headquarters in Manila, Philippines. As of September of 2003, the ADB had 58 member countries. Although ADB historically focused on government-level public agency lending with a governmental guarantee, the significant increase in privatizations in member countries has resulted in a private-sector mandate.

- **European Bank for Reconstruction and Development**   The European Bank for Reconstruction and Development (EBRD) began operations in 1991. It was organized to provide assistance to the nations of Central and Eastern Europe for transition to market based economies. There are over 50 member countries. The EBRD raises funds from member countries as well as the capital markets.

- **European Union**   The European Union, organized in 1993, is an organization of 25 industrialized European nations. It provides grants to developing countries throughout the world, including Africa, Asia, the Caribbean, central and eastern Europe, Latin America and the former Soviet Union.

- **European Investment Bank**   Organized in 1958, the European Investment Bank (EIB) provides financial support for development. The members of the EIB are the members states of the European Union. Funds are raised by the EIB from member countries and also from the capital markets. Loans are generally made within the European Union, but are also made outside of the union.

- **Inter-American Development Bank**   The Inter-American Development Bank (IDB) was organized in 1959, and is a major lender to Latin American and Caribbean member countries. It is currently the principal source of external finance for most Latin American countries. The 46 member countries include Latin American countries, the United States and other industrialized nations. Funds for loans are raised by the IDB from member countries as well as from the capital markets. Loans are generally made to public agencies of member countries to finance specific projects. A government guarantee is required. Direct support to the private sector is made available by the bank through its affiliate, the **Inter-American Investment Corporation (IIC)**.

- **Islamic Development Bank** The Islamic Development Bank (IsDB), established in 1974, is a multilateral organization of 45 countries. Its purpose is to promote economic development in member countries and in Muslim communities in non-member countries. The bank, operating within the principles of the Koran, provides interest-free loans for development projects, and also finances lease transactions and instalment sales, and makes equity investments.
- **Nordic Investment Bank** The Nordic Investment Bank (NIB) was formed in 1975 by Denmark, Finland, Iceland, Norway and Sweden. Its purpose is to finance investments in which its member nations are interested, both within the Nordic countries and internationally.
- **Nordic Development Fund** Since l989, the Nordic Development Fund (NDF) has provided credits to developing countries on concessional terms, primarily in Africa and Asia. It participates in co-financing arrangements with other multilateral agencies and regional banks.
- **OPEC Fund for International Development** The OPEC Fund for International Development, established in 1976, provides financial assistance to developing countries. Its members are the countries that are members of the Organization of Petroleum Exporting Countries.

Host governments

The host government is the government of the country in which the project is located. The host government is typically involved as an issuer of permits, licences, authorizations and concessions. It also might grant foreign exchange availability projections and tax concessions. In some projects, the host government is an owner of the project, whether majority or minority, or will become the owner of the project at the end of a specified period, such as in a build-own-transfer (BOT) structure. It might also be involved as an off-take purchaser or as a supplier of raw materials or fuel.

Construction contractors

These include the engineers and contractors responsible for designing and building the project. Any or all of these parties may be contractually part of the financing. The contractor is the entity responsible for construction of the project; to the extent construction of a facility is a part of the overall project. It bears the primary responsibility in most projects for the containment of construction-period costs.

Suppliers

Suppliers provide raw materials or other inputs to the project, since supply arrangements are key to project success, project sponsors and lenders are concerned with the underlying economic feasibility of supply arrangements and the supplier's ability to perform the contracts. Closely linked to inputs are the matter of appropriate transportation links and the ability to move the requisite materials or machinery through customs.

Purchasers

In large infrastructure projects, the project company will seek in advance to conclude long term agreements to sell the good or service being produced by the project (e.g. selling coal to electric power plants). This is known as an 'off-take agreement'. *The output purchaser* provide a crucial element of the credit support for the underlying financing by seeking to stabilize the acquisition of the raw materials over time and protect itself from market volatility. Such support can be seen as a credit enhancement (such as guarantees) to make the project more attractive to the financing banks.

Leasing companies

If capital allowances are available for the writing-down of plant and machinery or other assets, the project structure might involve one or more financial leasing companies. Their role will be to lease out assets to the project company in return for a rental stream. In addition to the tax advantages are the financial ones of keeping the assets off the project company's balance sheet.

Insurers

The sheer scale of many projects and the potential for incurring all sorts of liabilities dictates the necessity of arranging appropriate insurance arrangements. Insurers therefore play a crucial role in most projects. If there is a adverse incident affecting the project then the sponsor and the lenders will look to the insurers to cover them against loss.

Financing sources used in project financing

Just as financial instruments range from debt to equity and hybrids such as mezzanine finance, project finance can raise capital from a range of sources.

Raising financing depends on the nature and structure of the project financing being proposed. Lender and investor interest will vary depending on these goals and risks related to the financing. Commercial lenders seek projects with predictable political and economic risks. Multilateral institutions, on the other hand, will be less concerned with commercial lending criteria and will look towards projects that ostensibly satisfy not only purely commercial criteria.

In assembling a project financing, all available financing sources should be evaluated. This would include equipment suppliers with access to export financing; multilateral agencies; bilateral agencies, which may provide financing or guarantees; the International Finance Corporation or regional development banks that have the ability to mobilize commercial funds; specialized funds; institutional lenders and equity investors; and commercial banks, both domestic and international.

Equity

Equity is often raised in the stock markets and from specialized funds. Equity, as it is well known, is more expensive than debt financing. Domestic capital markets provide access to significant amounts of funds for infrastructure projects, although capital markets in developing countries may lack the depth to fund large transactions. In such cases, the international capital markets can also provide access to significant amounts of funds for infrastructure projects. However, this is generally limited to transactions whose sponsors are large, multinational companies. Access to international capital markets by companies in developing countries is generally limited, due to their low name visibility in the international financial markets.

Developmental loan

A development loan is debt financing provided during a project's developmental period to a sponsor with insufficient resources to pursue development of a project. The developmental lender is typically a lender with significant project experience. Developmental lenders, who fund the project sponsor at a very risky stage of the project, desire some equity rewards for the risk taken. Hence, it is not unusual for the developmental lender to secure rights to provide permanent financing for the project as part of the development financing arrangement.

Developmental loans are typically advanced to the project sponsor on a periodic basis, based on a budget prepared to cover the development stage of the project. The developmental lender will typically require liens on all project assets including project contracts. Repayment of the loan is typically from proceeds of construction financing. Developmental loans are extremely risky for the lender since there is no assurance that the project can be developed. These loans are also risky because the value of the collateral is totally dependent on the ability to complete the project. That value can reduce to nothing at any point.

Subordinated loans

Subordinated loans, also called mezzanine financing or quasi-equity, are senior to equity capital but junior to senior debt and secured debt. Subordinated debt usually has the advantage of being fixed rate, long term, unsecured and may be considered as equity by senior lenders for purposes of computing debt to equity ratios.

Subordinated debt can sometimes be used advantageously for advances required by investors, sponsors or guarantors to cover construction cost over-runs or other payments necessary to maintain debt to equity ratios, or other guaranteed payments.

Senior debt

Commercial banks and institutional lenders are an obvious choice for financing needs. Commercial banks tend to limit their commitments to 5–10 with floating interest rates based on LIBOR or US prime rate. Fixed interest rate loans for 5- to 10-year maturities or longer are sometimes available. Commercial bank loans for large projects are typically arranged as syndicated bank loans.

The senior debt of a project financing usually constitutes the largest portion of the financing and is usually the first debt to be placed. Generally the senior debt will be more than 50% of the total financing. Senior debt is debt that is not subordinated to any other liability, in other words, the first to be paid out if the company or project is placed under liquidation.

Senior debt falls into two categories: unsecured and secured loans.

Unsecured loans

Unsecured loans basically depend on the borrower's general credit-worthiness, as opposed to a perfected security arrangement. Unsecured loans will usually contain a negative pledge of assets to prohibit the liquid and valuable assets of the company from being pledged to a third party ahead of the unsecured lender.

The loan agreement may include ratio covenants and provisions calculated to trigger a security agreement, should the borrower's financial condition begin to deteriorate. An unsecured loan agreement may also contain negative covenants which limit investments and other kinds of loans, leases debt obligations of the borrower.

The loan agreement may also include affirmative covenants which are things that the company has to do: e.g. ensure that the business will be properly managed, proper books and records will be kept, financial information will be furnished, insurance coverage kept in force, and the business operated according to law.

Large unsecured loans are available only to the most creditworthy companies with long histories of commercially successful operation and good relationships with their lenders. Since projects tend to be new enterprises with no operating histories, projects rely upon the reputations of their sponsors, owners, and managers for standing in the financial community.

Secured loans

Secured loans are loans where the assets securing the loan have value as collateral, which means that such assets are marketable and can readily be converted into cash.

In a fully secured loan, the value of the asset securing the debt equals or exceeds the amount borrowed. The reputation and standing of the project managers and sponsors, and the probable success of the project, all enter into the lending decision. The lending, however, also relies on the value of the collateral as a secondary source of repayment. The security interest is regarded by lenders as protection of loan repayment in the unlikely event the loan is not repaid in the ordinary course of business. Because of the security interest, a secured loan is superior since it ranks ahead of unsecured debt. In the event of financial difficulties, the secured creditor in control of key assets of a project is in a position to demand that its debt service, payments of interest and principal continue, even if this means that unsecured creditors may be left with nothing.

The enforceability of security interests requires a practical word of caution. Inexperienced lenders sometimes confuse the right to realize security with the ability to realize it. It is important to distinguish between the two since the ability to enforce a right can come up against technical and practical difficulties of doing so – especially in the case of seizing properties located in countries with underdeveloped legal systems.

Syndicated loans

As we noted, project finance typically occurs in two phases: construction and operation. In some circumstances, the construction and operation phases are governed by separate agreements:

- **The construction phase** begins when the lender disburses funds for the construction of the project (as per the construction agreement, contingent on the submission of appropriate drawdown requests with supporting documentation such as completion certificates). Since there is no operating revenue during this stage, interest is typically capitalized.
- **The operations phase** begins when the construction is complete. The lending banks will advance funds (as per the terms in the loan agreement), typically on the first day of commercial operations. Since the project is now ostensibly generating a cash flow, payments of interest and principle can begin. The loan amortization schedule will have been drafted beforehand based on the cash flow projections, actual payments will of course depend on the actual cash flow generated. To account for minor variations in cash flow generation, the lenders may extend a working capital line of credit. Major shortfalls may lead to the loan facility being restructured.

A syndicated loan is a loan that is provided to the borrower by two or more banks, known as participants, which is governed by a single loan agreement. The loan is arranged and structured by an arranger and managed by an agent. The arranger and the agent may also be participants. Each participant provides a defined percentage of the loan, and receives the same percentage of repayments.

The syndicated lending market is international by nature – that is to say, many of the borrowers and projects being financed are international – taking place in Europe, Eastern Europe, Africa, the Middle East, etc. Furthermore, in order to place these large loans (e.g. up to several hundred million dollars) in the market, sometimes several banks are needed to participate in these loans.

The factors which account for the size and spectacular growth of this market are several:

- The market is international rather than being confined to a particular country, and new debt issues can avoid a great deal of national regulation which may involve onerous registration requirements. This can lead to a significant reduction in the cost of the issue.
- The international syndicated lending market has evolved a very fast, efficient and flexible distribution network which can place deals in large volumes and for the most part can ensure that they are launched successfully and in an orderly fashion.
- This is because syndicated loans are managed, underwritten and sold by syndicates. These syndicates are dominated by the London based Swiss, American, European, and Japanese banks which have access to large client bases.
- The international marketplace gives borrowers access to a greater number and diversity of investors than would be possible within their own marketplace. This ability to tap different sources of finance can reduce overall interest costs.
- The most important European banking markets are based in the UK. The effect of London being the UK's capital (capitol) city should not be overestimated. The large volume of activities, the variety and innovation of banking products, the large number of people employed in the UK banking industry is significantly influenced by the strength of the London trading and capital market activities.

The syndicated loan market was initially developed in London by a relatively small number of merchant banks which had small balance sheets but large and important customers. It would not have been possible for these merchant banks to provide the full amounts of loans needed by their customers and so other banks were asked to provide parts of the loans on the same terms and conditions, with the merchant bank taking a fee to arrange the loan and administer it once it was drawn. In today's terms, the merchant bank was acting as arranger and agent.

During the 1960s many North American and other foreign banks opened branches in London, attracted by the growth of the new Eurodollar market.

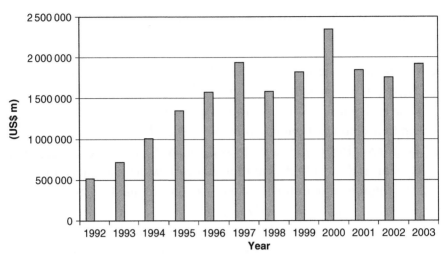

Figure 1.4   Global syndicated loan borrowing

These new branches could gain assets quickly and easily by participating in syndicated loans to borrowers with which they would not otherwise have had a relationship. The American and Japanese banks in particular began targeting large companies with the specific intention of arranging syndicated loans in order to maximize their fee income. In recent years in the London market, the part played by Japanese banks as arrangers has lessened and some of the UK clearing banks have become increasingly active.

Today the syndicated loan market is a major part of the operations of banks throughout the world, with major centres in London, New York and Hong Kong. They are typically used to finance large projects such as the Jorf Lasfar Power Station in Morocco – one of the largest syndicated loans.

World Bank group financing sources

Multilateral institutions such as the World Bank provide funds to infrastructure development projects world wide according to criteria which may change over time. While such financial support is limited, any involvement by these institutions is helpful to a project as it serves to 'validate' it in the eyes of banks which may be invited to participate in a

Table 1.2 Mandated arranger rankings for global syndicated loans, 1 January 2003 to 31 December 2003

Ranking	Bank name	Amt US$ m	No.	% share
1	Citigroup Inc	198 227	742	10.49
2	JP Morgan	193 678	824	10.24
3	Bank of America Corp	164 455	1048	8.70
4	Deutsche Bank AG	82 513	355	4.36
5	Barclays	80 827	328	4.28
6	Bank One	68 080	540	3.60
7	BNP Paribas	66 660	360	3.53
8	ABN AMRO	60 386	437	3.19
9	HSBC	59 810	284	3.16
10	Wachovia Corp	52 642	587	2.78
11	Royal Bank of Scotland	47 655	244	2.52
12	Mizuho	45 580	281	2.41
13	Credit Agricole – Credit Lyonnais	42 894	259	2.27
14	FleetBoston	40 474	449	2.14
15	Mitsubishi Tokyo Financial Group Inc	38 699	325	2.05
16	Credit Suisse First Boston	37 550	166	1.99
17	Sumitomo Mitsui Banking Corp	35 645	363	1.89
18	Dresdner Kleinwort Wasserstein	32 293	91	1.71
19	SG	30 156	178	1.60
20	UBS	17 927	97	0.95

parallel syndicated loan facility. Some of the World Bank's financing programmes are:

- **Loan Programme** Loans are generally made to member countries to finance specific projects. Eligibility is conditioned on a showing that the borrower is unable to secure a loan for the project from any other source on reasonable terms. It is therefore generally considered as the lender of last resort. Also, a showing must be made that the project is technically and economically feasible, and that the loan can be repaid.
- **Guarantee Programme** The World Bank also provides guarantees. After the debt crisis of the 1980s, and the decrease in commercial loans

in developing countries, guarantee programmes were established to improve access to financing sources. The World Bank Partial Risk Guarantee Program provides private sector lenders with limited protection against risks of sovereign non-performance and against certain force majeure risks.

■ **Indirect support**　World Bank involvement in a project can be extremely important, even though the financial commitment is small, as it basically confirms that the loan has met the World Bank's lending and financial analysis criteria and therefore validates it in the eyes of commercial banks. A World Bank involvement therefore can affect the availability of funds from other, non-World Bank affiliated sources.

Export credit agencies

Export credit agencies use three methods to provide funds to an importing entity:

■ **Direct lending**　This is the simplest structure whereby the loan is conditioned upon the purchase of goods or services from businesses in the organizing country.

■ **Financial intermediary loans**　Here, the export–import bank lends funds to a financial intermediary, such as a commercial bank, that in turn loans the funds to the importing entity.

■ **Interest rate equalization**　Under an interest rate equalization, a commercial lender provides a loan to the importing entity at below-market interest rates, and in turn receives compensation from the export–import bank for the difference between the below-market rate and the commercial rate.

Bonds

In recent years, the use of the bond market as a vehicle for obtaining debt funds has increased. Bond financings are similar to commercial loan structure, except that the lenders are investors purchasing the borrower's bonds in a private placement or through the public debt market. The bond holders are represented by a trustee that acts as the agent and representative of the bondholders. Bond purchasers are generally the most conservative source of financing for a project. The main bond markets are in Germany, Japan, the United Kingdom and the United States.

Advantages of bonds

Financing via bonds offers several advantages:

- **Large and liquid market**   The public debt market provides project sponsors with access to a large and liquid market. In contrast, limited bank and institutional funds are available for international projects.
- **Longer term of debt**   The public debt market tolerates a longer average life for debt than does the private debt market. Commercial banks and some institutional investors have regulatory or internal restrictions on long term lending.
- **Less onerous terms**   Terms of public debt deals are less onerous and contain fewer restrictive covenants than do private debt deals.

Disadvantages of bonds

- **Regulatory oversight**   Public market deals in the USA require lengthy SEC registration processes.
- **Ratings**   Credit ratings are necessary. These are time-consuming to obtain and affect the structuring and risk allocation in project contracts.
- **Consents to changes to underlying project are difficult**   Amendments, changes, or restructurings of a project are extremely difficult to negotiate and complete because of the passive nature of the investment.
- **Excess liquidity**   Bond issues yield all the proceeds at once, while in a bank deal, funds are only drawn as needed during construction (although commitment fees are typically levied on undrawn funds). The company must therefore manage this excess liquidity to best effect.
- **Expensive transaction costs**   Transaction costs are very high for accessing the public debt markets. Consequently, transactions of less than $100 million cannot generally access this market.

Investment funds

Investment funds mobilize private sector funds for investment in infrastructure projects. These specialized funds may be sponsored by governments or the private sector and include:

- asset funds or income funds;
- investment management companies and venture capital providers;
- money market funds.

Institutional lenders

Institutional lenders include life insurance companies, pension plans, profit-sharing plans and charitable foundations. These entities can be a substantial source of funding, particularly in the United States.

Leasing companies

Leasing companies, which use tax benefits associated with equipment ownership, can offer attractively priced leases for equipment, contributing to the overall pool of financing.

Vendor financing of equipment

Many equipment manufacturers have financing programmes to encourage the sale of their machinery and equipment. Credit terms and criteria may therefore be relatively competitive.

Contractors

Contractors are rarely able to participate significantly in the long term financing of large projects due to the relatively modest size of their balance sheet. However, they can provide support via fixed price contracts (e.g. building a project facility without cost overruns).

Contractors can also assist their clients by providing advice on the financing of projects, since they have had considerable expertise in dealing with lenders, potential sponsors and various government agencies. They may also be able to suggest structures and methods for project financing based on their previous experience in similar projects.

Sponsors

Sometimes, a direct loan or advance by a sponsor is the only way in which the project can be financed. Such direct loans may also be necessary as a result of cost over-runs or other contingent liabilities that the sponsor has assumed. A loan is preferable to a capital contribution, since it is more easily repaid.

Sponsor loans can be at lower than market rates, moreover, some sponsors prefer to lend directly to a project rather than to guarantee a loan, because they view the credit exposure as being the same, but prefer to earn interest on their exposure.

Supplier financing

A supplier seeking a market for a product or a by-product which it produces is sometimes willing to subsidise construction, or guarantee debt of a facility that will use that product. This might, for example, be a steel plant that would use natural gas in the Middle East. The list of possible suppliers varies with each project.

In such cases, a loan is made to the supplier, and the supplier quotes financing terms to the purchaser. Supplier credits usually require the supplier to assume some of the financing risk, although in practical terms, the supplier's profit margin may exceed the risk assumed.

Host government

The host government can also be a direct or indirect source of financing.

■ Direct sources are when the government loans funds to the project company.

■ Indirect sources comprise tax relief, tax holidays, waiving customs duties for project equipment, etc.

There are a number of advantages to host country financing assistance in a project. These include reducing the impact of leverage; subordination; foreign exchange burden on the project sponsors. It also implies that the government support decreases political risk, which can help attract private capital.

Chapter 2

Understanding key project risks

Project finance is subject to several types of risks. It is useful therefore to look at these risks by category and identify their salient features and characteristics.

Entity risks

Each project finance participant has a different perspective on risk, often based on the role it is playing in the overall project financing structure. This perspective will obviously impact the participant's appetite for risk. The view of risk moreover is subjective and based not only on economic factors but on characteristics relating to the financial condition of the participant. A particular risk, event or condition that is unacceptable to one party may be considered manageable and routine by another. The identification of risks and knowledge of the participants is therefore essential if a project financing is to be assembled successfully. We will therefore consider the risk perspective of each participant in a project financing.

Sponsor

The project sponsor's objectives are based on the very reasons the project finance exists. Due to the complexity of project financings, the sponsor is interested in several objectives, such as limiting further development costs, minimizing transaction costs, recovering development stage expenses and earning construction, management, or similar fees to fund project company construction activities for the project. And in the long term, the sponsor is motivated with the cash flow generation potential of the project. The sooner the project financing comes on stream, the sooner the sponsor benefits from the revenues generated. Thus, the sponsor would want to mitigate any risks which might delay or prevent the project from coming on stream.

Construction lender

The construction lender in a project financing is concerned with the design engineering and construction risks, since completing the construction is necessary in order to enable the borrower to draw down the permanent financing and use it to repay the initial construction loan. More specifically, the construction lender will be concerned with provisions relating to timely completion and performance at expected levels.

Credit enhancement devices to increase the likelihood of repayment of the construction loan may need to be in place. Examples are completion guarantees and performance and payment bonds.

Permanent lender

The permanent lender needs to:

■ arrange sufficient debt to finance the total construction cost of the project;
■ ensure the absence of any other lender in a more senior collateral or control position;
■ conclude satisfactory intercreditor agreements if more than one lender is involved in the financing.

The permanent lender is generally concerned with the economic value of the project, and the legal adequacy of the contracts, and enforceability of the contracts in a loan workout scenario.

Overall, the lender attempts to structure a financing that ensures:

■ All costs before construction completion are without recourse to lender for additional funds.

- The contractor satisfies performance guarantees, as evidenced by performance tests.
- There is recourse to other creditworthy project participants for delay and completion costs if the project is abandoned and if minimum performance levels are not achieved.
- There are predictable revenue streams that can be applied to service debt.
- The revenue streams are long term, from a creditworthy source and in an amount that covers operating costs and debt service (e.g. an off-take agreement).
- The project maximizes revenue while minimizing costs, complying with environmental laws (or lobbying to obtain exemptions) in order to maintain long term viability.

Contractor

The relationship between the sponsor and contractor is based on the fact that the turnkey nature of the construction project requires the contractor to deliver the project on spec and on time. This means that the contractor is concerned with the difficulty of predicting events that could adversely impact the parameters of the project and avoiding them. There are certain methods of incentivizing the contractor; for example, increasing the construction price or via a bonus payment in the case of early completion. The contractor is also concerned with the underlying financing documents, including whether the sponsor has arranged sufficient financing to pay the contractor for work performed.

Operator

The relationship between the project sponsor and operator is concerned with the need for price and performance predictability of the project. While the other project participants will want to ensure that the operating costs are fixed or predictable so that debt servicing ability can be analysed, the operator, in contrast, wants to limit price risk.

The operator can address this risk by agreeing to operate the project according to a budget approved by the project company. The operator moreover agrees to operate the project within the parameters of the agreed-upon performance levels, and according to laws and industry practice.

Supplier

Suppliers are concerned with the challenges of providing requisite raw materials for the project and seek in return a fair and stable market price. Project participants on the other hand are concerned with quality and timely delivery of the raw materials with minimum price fluctuations.

Off-taker/purchaser

The off-taker is concerned with firm price and quality, and with minimum uncertainty. The project company, in contrast, wants to increase prices as the market will permit, and to be excused from performance failures (without penalties) for limited periods.

Host government

The project can offer the government short term and long term benefits from the project.

■ Short term, the government can use the project for political benefits and for attracting other developers to a country.
■ Long term, the successful project should improve economic prosperity and, perhaps, political stability, by providing the needed infrastructure, that is, if funds are not siphoned off by the ruling nomenklatura into offshore bank accounts.

It is therefore normal that the host country assume some of the project risks. This is particularly important for large high-profile projects. For example, implementation agreements, negotiated and executed with the host government, can provide a variety of government assurances with respect to the project risks. The host government might be involved in a project in one or several ways. These include as equity contributor, debt provider, guarantee provider (particularly political risks), supplier of raw materials and other resources, output purchaser and provider of fiscal support (reduced import fees, tax holidays and other incentives).

The host government also has an ongoing role. It can ensure a smooth regulatory climate in future by ensuring permit compliance and through regulatory structures.

Other governments

A project might require the cooperation of third countries for project success. For example, the project may depend on a steady supply of fuel from a third country. Or the project production may need to be exported to a foreign country, thus necessitating the appropriate permits and contractual commitments. It is therefore essential that such interrelations be identified so that they can be managed within an appropriate legal and documentary framework.

Equity investor

Equity investors make a risk analysis similar to lenders. The structuring goals are quite different, however. Project lenders hold a first priority security interest on all project assets, want sufficient project revenues generated to service operating expenses, pay debt service and maintain other requisite reserve accounts, and pay dividends. Equity investors, on the other hand, may share some of these goals but will focus on receiving dividends regularly, keep reserve account balances to a minimum, and maintain a potential residual value in the project after the debt is paid off.

Multilateral and bilateral agencies

Multilateral and bilateral agencies have similar perspectives, but moreover must factor in political and government funding constraints. Each entity has separate charters and goals which define precisely the perspectives each has in a project.

Export credit agencies (ECAs) obviously have a political focus – to stimulate exports, whilst multilateral banks have a focus of providing long term loans on soft terms.

Transaction risks

The essence of any project financing is the identification of all key risks associated with the project and the apportionment of those risks among the various parties participating in the project. Without a detailed analysis of these project risks at the outset, the parties do not have a clear understanding of what obligations and liabilities they may be assuming in connection with the project and therefore they are not in a position to consider appropriate risk-mitigation exercises at the relevant time.

Should problems arise when the project is under way, it can result in considerable delays, large expenses and arguments as to who is responsible. As a general rule, a particular risk should be assumed by the party best able to manage and control that risk.

Due to the complexity, each project will have a different risk profile, that is, each project will have different kinds of risks and the magnitude of risks will differ from project to project. In general, however, there are some major areas of risks which should be addressed in every project so that they can be mitigated properly. We treat the main category of risks in this section below.

Preliminary risk assessment

Feasibility studies

The feasibility study is a useful mechanism for setting forth a description of the project, the goals of the project sponsor, sensitivities of the project to various construction, start-up and operating risks, an analysis of financing alternatives and credit enhancement. It will include estimated capital needs, debt service capabilities, revenue projections from output sales, operating costs and market projections. Typically, variables such as fuel cost fluctuation, interest rates, currency exchange rates and others are examined in alternative scenarios.

The study enables the sponsor and lenders to analyse the potential of the project before any party unnecessarily commits resources when the project is not economically feasible. The study must, of course, conclude that the project will have sufficient viability to pay debt service, operations and maintenance costs provide a return on equity, and, if necessary, provide for contingencies. The feasibility study is useful in that it can be analysed by various legal, financial and technical experts to establish whether the project if viable or not.

Due diligence

Due diligence in project financing is an important process for risk identification. It encompasses legal, technical, environmental and financial matters, and is designed to detect events that might result in total or partial project failure. Participants involved in this process, besides the project sponsors, are lawyers, construction companies, fuel consultants, market consultants, insurance consultants, financial advisers and environmental consultants. The level of due diligence undertaken involves considerations of time available, cost and the type of project.

Risk periods

There are three main risk periods in a project financing:

- engineering and construction;
- start-up;
- operational.

Figure 2.1 shows how the risks increase throughout this phase. The lenders become more exposed as funds are drawn down but until the start-up and operation phase there is no certainty that the project will succeed.

Engineering and construction phase risks

This first stage is when the risk is highest – funds begin to flow from the financiers to the project entity. No cash flow is being generated from the project, however, so no interest can be paid and in many financings

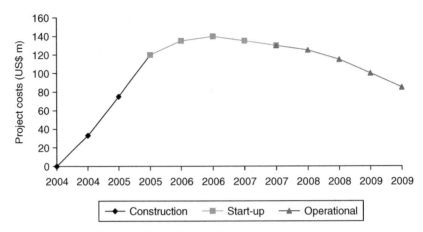

Figure 2.1 Risk phases and project costs

the borrower is allowed to 'roll up' interest or draw down further funds to make interest payments. The length of this phase can vary from several months (for example, the construction of a short toll road) to several years (for example, the construction of the Channel Tunnel). The lenders become more exposed as funds are drawn down but cash flows have yet to be generated.

Risks associated with the project during the construction phase include:

- **Sponsor risk**   Sponsor risk is closely associated with completion risk. The bank's view on completion risk will be strongly influenced by their view on sponsor risk, which may be broken down into two elements: Equity commitment and corporate strength and experience, also called 'corporate substance' Regarding equity commitment, lenders will normally require a contribution of anything from 15% to 50% of the project cost to ensure the sponsor's continued commitment. In addition, lenders prefer to work with corporate sponsors that have substantial technical expertise and financial depth.
- **Pre-completion risk**   The engineering and design review focuses on the suitability of the technology and design chosen for the project. These objectives recognize that construction risk levels vary among different technologies and the size of certain projects. Banks may well hesitate to finance projects using unproven technology.

- **Siting and permitting** Site and permitting risks are often linked to political risk, and can present a more difficult area of analysis. Regulations and legislation in some jurisdictions can leave continuous openings for project opponents to stop projects for reasons related, or unrelated, to siting concerns.
- **Completion risks** In essence, the risk is whether or not the project can be built on time, on budget and in accordance with the applicable specifications and design criteria.
- **Experience and resources of contractor** The contractor's experience, reputation and reliability should provide an indicator of the possibility of achieving timely completion of the project at the stated price. In projects, especially international projects, elements to analyse include human and technical resources necessary to satisfy contractual requirements, as well as ability to work with the local labour force.
- **Building materials** A project finance risk often overlooked. Of particular concern is the impact of import and export laws when the project is either located abroad or where imported materials are contemplated for construction.
- **Facility site** Pre-existing conditions on the project site can affect both construction and long term operations, especially if the site has hazardous waste problems.
- **Construction of related facilities** International projects, particularly in developing countries, often require simultaneous construction of facilities related to the project. These various facilities will all be interrelated and may need simultaneous construction to ensure project success. It is therefore important to analyse construction synchronization, since this may be the most important initial concern to the promoters of the underlying project.
- **Cost overruns** The risk that construction costs start to increase uncontrollably is perhaps the most important risk for the participants in a project financing. This may result in liquidity crises, as well as impact on long term cash flows.
- **Completion delays** Construction delays can have a similar impact to cost overruns, as it may affect the scheduled flow of project revenues necessary to cover debt service and operations and maintenance expenses, and result in higher than expected financing costs.

Start-up risks

During the start-up phase the banks need to be satisfied that the project will operate at the costs and according to the specifications agreed at the outset. The phase is especially significant if the loan becomes 'non-recourse' once the project has been completed (this is known as 'conversion').

The basis on which conversion takes place will require much thought and negotiation prior to the loan being signed. At this point, however, it is important to understand that the start-up phase may last for a period of many months. The technical assessment of a project therefore includes an evaluation of the facility's acceptance testing and start-up procedures, since they are an integral part of construction completion.

A potential conflict of interest and therefore risk arises from the need to start commercial operations versus the need to get the project to pass its long term reliability test. Financial pressures, which often occur near the end of the construction phase, to 'get the job done' may prompt the sponsor to accept a compromised performance test in an effort to generate cash flow as soon as possible. This is why lenders typically require that the engineer who engineer witnesses, verifies and signs off on all testing before releasing the contractor be fully independent (the engineer can, of course, be subjected to bribes or other pressures).

Operational risks

Once the project is complete the lenders in many project financings become dependent on stable cash flows to service the project loans. The lending risk is similar to the risks encountered in commercial loans in similar businesses. The future cash flows of the project company are subject to the usual operating costs, raw material costs, regulatory risks and markets for the products. The lenders can protect themselves by requiring the project company to maintain ratios and loan covenants: working capital, dividends and build-up of cash.

- **Operating/performance risk**   Operational risk is the risk that normal ongoing operations will fail to generate the cash flow required to run the project and service debt. This is why banks tend to be reassured if the project operations will be taken on by experienced third party operations and maintenance contractors, on a fixed cost basis. The main concern to lenders therefore is whether the project company has the experience and resources to manage the project, and if not, whether third parties, with sufficient creditworthiness to mitigate the risk of default, can.

■ **Raw material/supply risk**   This is another key risk category: input and supply risk relates to obtaining the requisite energy and raw materials for the project. The flow of these inputs must be assured, and within the parameters set by the project financial projections. This is why it is important to identify alternate sources should they be needed. Moreover, elements such as import or export fees, transportation charges, storage costs, can adversely impact the cost basis of these inputs. These factors should be factored into the financial projections in order to reassure the lenders that appropriate cash flow exists to meet operating costs and debt servicing commitments.

■ **Off-take and sales risk**   The off-take and sales risk is the risk that the project will fail to generate sufficient cash flow. This is why the sales, or off-take risk, is the key risk that banks will look at. Off-take agreements such as long term contracts to purchase electricity at fixed prices will substantially eliminate any sales volatility or instability, and will be considered as a positive element by the banks. Banks may therefore require the project sponsors to obtain off-take agreements, which leads to more basic questions such as: Is there a ready market for the project's products? How are the products going to be transported to market? Lenders will want to have the proper structures in place to insulate them from any potentially adverse effects arising from delays in the transportation process.

■ **Counterparty risk**   Counterparties include parties such as the contractor, bank providing bonds, purchasers or off-takers, insurance companies, etc. If any of these parties defaults in the performance of their respective obligations, then the project may run into difficulties. This raises three potential difficulties: The first is that a potential default risk exists, the second is that if such a risk arises, there is a potential documentation risk, which may be expensive and time-consuming to sort out, and the third is that since damages based claims are unliquidated claims, basic common law damages rules may apply in common law based jurisdictions, which affect the value of such claims.

■ **Technology/obsolescence risk** Banks tend to want to avoid new technology risk until it becomes proven technology. However, project sponsors cannot ignore new technology since often the success of such projects resides in cost efficiencies arising from new technology. Therefore, as a minimum, the contractor must have experience with the technology and provide adequate guarantees to support the underlying debt.

Financial risks

The project is now operating as a regular operating company and cash flow are being generated. As long as the project is performing according to plan, the risks to the lenders will reduce from their peak in the start-up phase. The borrower should not only be able to make interest payments but also repay the principal. As long as correct financial planning has been carried out, the company should be in a position to service debt. In a typical project finance transaction the banks will ensure that they have security over the sales proceeds.

Once the project is on stream, the project financial advisers should identify and mitigate for any risks that may occur outside of the project and scope of the project sponsor's control. Some of these risks are:

■ **Foreign exchange (FX) risk** If all project inputs are denominated on one currency, there will be no FX risk. If this is not the case, the lender may need to assume some of the risk via multi-currency loans which give the borrower an option, based on a fixed FX rate, of repaying in different currencies. Lenders can sometimes hedge these risks using appropriate hedging instruments.

■ **Interest rate risk** Project financings may rely on floating interest rate loans. Most project financings remove interest rate risk by financing with fixed interest rate debt. Some projects however have incorporated debt with interest rates tied to a floating reference rate. Where projects chose to use floating rate debt, the financial projections should demonstrate that in a high interest rate scenario the project will still have enough available cash flow to service financing commitments.

■ **Inflation risk** This risk exists when certain of the inputs can be subjected to price inflation (e.g. rising fuel costs). In such cases, the project sponsor must be able to pass on these price increases to customers. If the project output is a product whose price levels are fixed by the government (e.g. electricity cost), the ability to pass on the cost increase will be limited. Similar risks exist when the inputs are denominated in one currency and the project outputs in another. Thus it is important to identify any such risks and the ability to pass them on to the customers.

■ **Liquidity risk** Projects should be able to demonstrate the ability to generate sufficient cash to fund major maintenance reserve funds. If not, a potential liquidity risk exists. Financial projections should therefore demonstrate that an adequate cash flow, enabling the company to generate enough cash to fund ongoing operations and fund reserves, exists. In some cases, project financings allocate a specific working capital facility for this purpose.

■ **Product pricing** In the absence of off-take contracts, the lender needs to analyse the likely market price of the good or service being provided and evaluate the likelihood that the price levels achieved will suffice to cover operating costs and debt servicing requirements.

Country/political risks

Consider the following definition of country risk, provided by P. Nagy:

> *Country risk is the exposure to a loss in cross-border lending caused by events in a particular country which are, at least to some extent, under the control of the government but definitely not under the control of a private enterprise or individual.*

When analysing this definition, one can find that country risk can arise through different paths. Indeed three types of events can cause country risk:

■ Political events such as war, ideology, neighbouring countries, political unrest, revolution, etc. comprise political risk. Political risk is the risk that a country is not willing or able, due to political reasons, to service/repay its foreign debt/obligations.

- Economic factors such as internal and external debt levels, GDP growth, inflation, import dependency etc. comprise economic risk. Economic risk is the risk that a country is not willing or able, due to economic reasons, to service/repay its foreign debt/obligations.
- Social factors such as religious, ethnic, or class conflict, trade unions, inequitable income distribution etc. comprise social risk. Social risk is the risk that a country is not able, or is unwilling, to repay its foreign debt/obligations due to social reasons.

Therefore, when we speak about country risk, we mean the exposure to a loss in cross-border lending (of different types) due to events more or less under the control of the government.

Typical examples of political risk are:

- expropriation or nationalization of project assets;
- failure of a government department to grant a necessary consent or permit;
- imposition of increased taxes and tariffs;
- withdrawal of valuable tax holidays and/or concessions;
- imposition of exchange controls, restricting the transfer of funds to outside the host country;
- changes in law adversely impacting project parties' obligations with respect to the project.

Political stability is an important ingredient for cross-border project financing success.

In project financing, the political risks are more acute because:

- The project may rely on governmental concessions, licences or permits.
- Tariffs, quotas or prohibitions might be imposed on exports of the project's production.
- The host government might introduce controls to restrict the rate of production or depletion of the project's reserves, either for national

reasons to do with the management of the host government's economy or for international reasons such as compliance with OPEC quotas.

■ Additional taxes might be imposed on the project's production, such as the surcharge taxes imposed by the United Kingdom on revenues from North Sea oil production.

Legal risks

By legal risk is meant that the application of laws in the host country may not necessarily be consistent with that of the lender's home countries, and that judgements may yield results substantially different than those expected. It is therefore essential that project lenders review the legal risks at an early stage. Some banks may require the host country to pass specific legislation favourable to a project, which lends a new meaning to 'interference in domestic affairs'! Getting such legislation implemented no doubt requires numerous cash commissions to key government officials to accelerate lengthy procedures. A breakdown of legal risks includes:

■ **Identifying and establishing applicable laws and jurisdiction** Project finance requires the establishment of a stable legal framework required for ongoing business operation. It is therefore important to identify the strengths and weaknesses of a given legal system and plan for the shortcomings appropriately.

■ **Security** In a project finance – particularly where recourse is limited – the ability to take effective security can assume crucial importance. Laws on the taking and enforcement of security, particularly in the case of moveable assets, cash flows and contractual rights (such as receivables) might be less than satisfactory, and should be evaluated.

■ **Permits and licensing** There is a risk when permits and licences must be obtained and renewed before the plant will operate. Effectively, this means that the lenders are assuming the risk that the requisite permits and licenses will be obtained in a reasonable time should the sponsors not provide any commitment to assume the costs arising from such delays.

■ **Limited rights to appeal** The local lawyers and the judiciary might lack the requisite experience to judge project related disputes; resulting judgements may therefore be slower than expected and, yield unpredictable results.

- **Enforceability of contracts**   Even if a project is supported by take-or-pay contracts with adequate escalation clauses, enforceability may very well be an open question, as well as the ability or motivation of the contracting party to honour its contractual commitments.
- **Structural risk**   This is the risk that the interrelations of project elements may not function as initially envisaged. Complex projects can involve complex and interlocking documents which may be flawed. Allegiances moreover can shift during the life of a contract.

Environmental, regulatory and approval risks

Obtaining all the requisite approvals for a project is indispensable to its success. Indeed, all permissions should be obtained prior to setting in place the facility and forwarding funds. It is essential that these be included as conditions precedent in the facility documentation. Likewise for environmental and regulatory issues: these should be spelled out clearly in the loan agreement since there is a risk that other regulatory and environmental risks, may live to haunt the lenders if the project should fail and decontamination costs have to be borne by the lender who takes possession of the security in order to satisfy the outstanding loan.

- **Environmental risk**   Environmental risk is increasingly becoming an issue of public concern, and is increasingly being subject to legislation controlling the adverse impact projects and the emissions, waste, hazardous substances and inefficient use of energy they may generate. Lenders need to insulate themselves from these risks. Some methods are to:
  - Understand the relevant legal framework in the host country and its impact on project feasibility.
  - Evaluate the risks relating to the project site, supplies, transportation from the site, and the products, emissions and waste that the project will generate.
  - Ensure that satisfaction of the relevant environmental and regulatory issues are a condition precedent to making finance available, including ensuring that the project will be able to meet future tightening of environmental controls.

- Documentation should contain representations, warranties and covenants on the borrower's part to ensure compliance with these issues.
- Monitor the project on an ongoing basis to ensure that the project operates within required environmental parameters.
- **Regulatory, licensing and permit risks**   It is essential that all regulatory, licensing and permits issues are met at the outset of the project since if there are any difficulties and the lenders take possession of the security when a project fails to perform, this may cause difficulties. In the absence of appropriate governmental permits, this may result in fines. In the case of regulatory and licensing issues, the lenders may find themselves liable for the legal consequences of pollution caused by that project. The position is more ambiguous in other countries but bankers are concerned that the increasing profile of environmental issues might increase the risks of banks assuming these responsibilities in the event of pollution claims arising from their borrowers.
- **Public opposition**   Public opposition to a project can become an unwelcome nuisance to bankers. Public opposition (via procedural challenges of permits and approvals) can result in costly delays to the project. The feasibility study should therefore consider public opposition as one factor in the chance for project success.

Refinancing risk

The repayment of construction financing by long term financing means that the former is depending on the latter for 'takeout'. This is known as refinancing risk, as it assumes repayment of the former by extension of the latter. The solution to this is to arrange the latter upon the signing of the former. This however is not always possible since there are often long lead times in a project. Construction lenders can try to protect themselves by providing incentives to sponsors to arrange the long term debt (e.g. gradually escalating interest rates, by triggering additional sponsor guarantees, or by requiring a takeout by the sponsor, since project financings tend to have the same group of lenders for both construction lending and long term lending). Repayment risk therefore needs to be evaluated on a case by case basis.

Force majeure

Force majeure means that entities are not responsible for performance shortfalls caused by unanticipated events outside their control. Project finance transactions are particularly vulnerable to force majeure risks due to the complexity of the transactions, the numerous participants in the project, the physical nature of construction activity, associated technical and performance risks, and impact of geographic distance and transport of raw materials.

Sponsors typically will not want to assume those risks and the financing parties should not accept these risks (in addition to the credit risks already assumed). It is therefore important to segregate risks which are those under the borrower's remit (technical, construction) against natural risks (floods and earthquakes, civil disturbances, strikes, or changes of law). While companies may be exempt from force majeure risks, it should be noted that they may still lead to a default depending on its severity.

The unpredictability of force majeure events makes effective mitigation difficult. Projects that show linearity in design or operations, such as toll roads, pipelines, or assembly line production, tend to be less at risk of operational force majeure accidents than operations which are complex (e.g. chemical plants, LNG facilities, refineries, and nuclear power plants). It is therefore essential that the project be assed in light of such risks so that facility pricing and structure is commensurate with the risk profile of the project and downside cash flow analyses be undertaken to assess how much resistance the project structure has to such vicissitudes.

Lender liability risk

Lender liability risk may not be directly related to the project. Lenders however should be aware of this risk. One aspect of lender liability is the exercise of 'undue control' by a lender intervening in the customer's business by taking actions associated with ownership or management. Undue control can make the lender liable for the consequences if the borrower becomes insolvent. The need to draw a fine line between unacceptable 'control' and careful 'credit monitoring' is particularly acute in the context of project finance.

Excessive restrictions imposed on the borrower's operations, the reporting and monitoring of progress, the control of disbursements and receivables, and the insistence on comprehensive security packages, increase the likelihood that the lender might be regarded as having an active role in the conduct of the business.

Conversely, banks in the United States have also been held responsible for the financial consequences of *failing* to make loans after entering into a commitment to lend.

There are a number of ways in which lenders can try to reduce the risk of lender liability:

- Include carefully drafted covenants in the documentation. These should be drafted carefully to ensure that the lender is not seen to be effectively exercising control.
- Have these restrictions expressed as events of default, rather than as proactive directions to follow specific policies.
- Avoid taking an equity interest in the borrower and/or in having a nominee director on its board.
- Take minutes during meetings with the project sponsors and borrower, to minimize the risk of allegations of misrepresentation or failure to negotiate in good faith.
- Make finance offers subject to final documentation and to be indicative, rather than exhaustive, of the terms and conditions of the offer.
- Make events of default specific and subject to objective tests rather than dependent on the discretion of the lender.
- Ensure that the financial covenants cannot be construed as the imposition of a 'business plan' on the borrower (e.g. use financial ratios, and not specific project related mileposts).
- Phrase management change covenants such that a 'change of management constitutes an event of default', rather than state that they are 'prohibited from changing management'.

Particular care should be taken in loan defaults or reschedulings: if the lenders take advantage of the borrower's weakened condition and try to impose corrective measures, this may render the lenders liable for the borrower's obligations since they will be deemed to have taking a pro-active role in the management of the borrower's ongoing operations.

Mitigating and managing project risks

Construction and completion risks

Completion risks can be allocated or mitigated in the following ways:

- **Turnkey contract** Turnkey arrangements are popular with lenders since they avoid gaps appearing in the contract structure and disputes between the subcontractors as to where particular risks lie. Lenders will prefer that the contractor assume responsibility for the design element of the works, thus simplifying negotiations with only one party for all aspects of the construction works during the construction period.
- **Fixed price lump sum contract** These reduce the likelihood of cost overruns being the responsibility of the project company. If there are to be any changes to the contract price, this will enable the lenders to protect their position, especially if there are any changes to project specifications by the project company.
- **Cost overrun** Cost overruns can be mitigated by contractual under-takings, e.g. the infusion of additional equity by the project sponsor, other equity participants, or standby equity participants. Similarly, standby funding agreements for additional financing, either from the construction lender or subordinated debt lent by project participants or third parties, can be used. This can be done by having the project sponsor create an escrow fund to provide liquidity in the case of cost overruns.
- **Completion guarantee** Pre-completion risks can be covered via the use of a completion guarantee. This is basically a guarantee from one or more of the project sponsors that the loan will be repaid if completion (as defined by certain performance tests) is not achieved by a certain date.
- **Completion test** Once the project has been completed, the sponsors will wish to be released from whatever undertakings they have made

to the lenders. The exact moment at which this happens is determined by the 'completion test'. The terms of the completion test usually involve considerable negotiation between lenders and sponsors. Completion can be defined by

- an architect's certificate of completion is issued (e.g. hotel);
- physical completion (provided by independent consultants);
- production test (production of a X over a particular period);
- sales contract: confirmation the borrower can meet the obligations of any supplier contracts it has signed;
- economics test: ability to profitably operate the facility as defined by cash flow coverage ratios incorporated in the loan agreement.
- **Liquidated damages in construction contracts**   If construction of a project is at a stage where commercial operations cannot be undertaken or the project does not operate after completion at guaranteed levels, the project company will still need to service debt and other obligations. This can occur via 'liquidated damage payments' – these constitute an estimate by the contractor and project sponsor of the shortfall arising from late or deficient performance. The advantage of the liquidated damage clause is to avoid calculation of damages following a dispute. Enforceability of a liquidated damage clause, however, must be carefully considered, particularly in the international context.

Operational risks

- **Long term supply contracts**   In many projects, long term requirements contracts are developed to provide the necessary raw material supply at a predictable price to reduce this risk. In such cases, the lender must ensure that the credit of the supplier be sufficient to ensure performance of the contract.
- **Take-or-pay contracts**   Project financiers can minimize cash flow risk by entering into 'take-or-pay' contracts. This is a contract entered into between the project company and a third party whereby the third party agrees to purchase a specified amount of the project's production over a specified period whether or not it actually takes delivery of them. The advantage to the project entity of course is that it locks in a portion of the production over time at a fixed price – which may

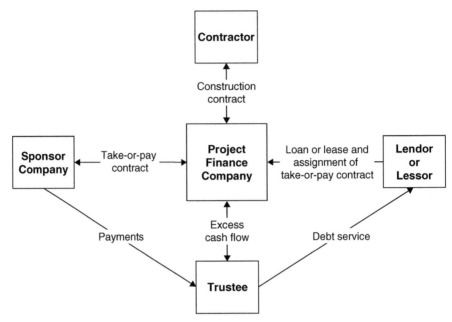

Figure 2.2 Project financing supported by a take-or-pay contract

Summary:
- A sponsor company enters into a take-or-pay contract with a project.
- A project company arranges a loan or lease with a lender or lessor and assigns the take-or-pay contract as security to the lender or lessor or to a security trustee acting for them.
- Proceeds of the loan or lease are used to finance the construction of the property.
- Take-or-pay contract payments are made to the trustee which, in turn, pays debt service to the lender(s) or lessor(s); any excess cash flow is paid to the project company.

be below prevailing market prices but which are stable and locked in over time, thereby facilitating financial planning. The incentive for the off-taker to enter such contracts is the desire to obtain certainty of supply in circumstances and at a price which otherwise might be unavailable to it. The bank's position is considerably strengthened by a take-or-pay contract, as it can ensure that the proceeds of such contracts be paid into the lending bank's account, an additional cash flow monitoring mechanism. Note that the off-take purchaser must be credit-worthy if such arrangements are to provide the requisite comfort to the bankers.

- **Take-and-pay contract**   A take-and-pay contract is similar to the take-or-pay contract except that the buyer is only obligated to pay if the

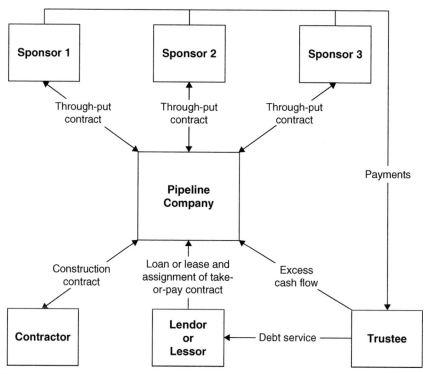

Figure 2.3 Project financing supported by a through-put contract
Summary:
- Three sponsor companies enter into a through-put contract with a pipeline company.
- The pipeline company enters into a loan or lease with a lender or lessor and assigns the through-put contract as security to the lender or lessor (or to a security trustee acting for them).
- Proceeds from the loan are used to build the pipeline.
- Payments under the through-put contract are paid to the trustee; the trustee uses those payments for debt service and pays the excess cash flow to the pipeline company.

product or service is actually delivered. Thus, a take-and-pay contract does not contain an unconditional obligation.

- **Throughput agreements** Throughput agreements usually apply to cases where there is an obligation to provide a service, such as the transmission of a product through a pipeline or number of cars on a railroad. The user will agree to supply minimum amounts of raw materials for processing and will pay tolling fees. These tolling fees should cover the debt-service obligations and other costs of the owner of the processing plant.

Financial risks

Financial risk can be reduced or mitigated through the use of derivative instruments. The risks that can be controlled are those associated with funding costs (interests), currency fluctuations when cash flows are not in the home currency and commodity price fluctuations. Examples of derivative instruments include: futures, forwards, options and swaps:

- **Futures contracts**   In a project financing, interest rate futures can be used to protect against funding costs and currency future to protect against foreign exchange rate fluctuations.
- **Forward contracts**   Forward contract on foreign exchange are used for hedging existing or anticipated currency exposures. Long term foreign exchange agreements can be used by project companies manage the currency risk arising from multi currency transactions.
- **Options**   A call option gives the buyer a maximum price (the strike price) and a put option gives the buyer a minimum price (the strike price) at which the underlying product can be sold. Project companies can therefore use calls and puts to control input and output prices. The cost of this protection naturally is equal to the option price.
- **Swaps**   Swaps can mitigate financial risks. There are currency swaps, interest rate swaps and commodity swaps. An interest rate swap can create a source of lower cost debt or higher yielding assets, and provide access to an otherwise unavailable source of funds. A commodity swap can be used to manage the price risk of the outputs or inputs for a project.

Political risks

It is impossible to mitigate all risks pertaining to a specific project. One way to avoid entering into potentially high risk lending situations, reducing political risk, is to lend through, or in conjunction with, multilateral agencies such as the World Bank, the EDRD and other regional development banks such as the ADB.

The rationale behind this is that when one or more of these agencies is involved in a project, the risk of an uncooperative or unhelpful attitude from the host country is reduced since the host government is unlikely to want to offend any of these agencies for fear of cutting off a valuable source of credit in the future. The default track record of Mexico and Brazil in the 1980s supports this view – whether it remains applicable 20 years later in different cultural and geographical contexts however, remains open to conjecture.

Other ways of protecting against political risk include:

- **Private market insurance**, although this can be expensive and subject to exclusions rendering the policy's effectiveness next to useless. More-over, the term that such insurance is available for will rarely be long enough.
- **Political insurance** from national export agencies (usually be given in connection with the export of goods and/or services by a supplier to the project). Lending in conjunction with national export credit agen-cies tends to probably enjoy a similar 'protected' status as loans in conjunction with development banks since there is a government ele-ment in addition to purely commercial element. Here, 'government involvement', not surprisingly, is seen as a reassuring accomplice rather than the realization of the 'government as the source of all evil and an infringement on capitalist freedom' arguments espoused by ideological zealots.
- **Obtaining assurances from the relevant government departments** in the host country, especially as regards the availability of consents and permits. This is only needed when the country is not having democracy imposed on it by hyperpowers waging extra-legal preemptive wars.
- **The central bank** may guarantee the availability of hard currency for export in connection with the project provided appropriate individuals are lobbied assiduously.
- **Thorough review of the legal and regulatory regime** in the country where the project is to be located is essential so as to ensure that all laws and regulations are complied with and all procedures are fol-lowed correctly, therefore reducing the scope for challenge at a future date. In countries with primitive legal systems and 'commission hungry' government officials, such ambiguities should be clearly identified in order to enable an accurate risk assessment and loan pricing mech-anism to be set in place.

Table 2.1 Government agencies providing political risk insurance

Australia	Export Finance and Insurance Corporation	EFIC
Austria	Osterreichische Kontrolibank AG	OKB
Belgium	Office National du Ducroire	OND
Canada	Export Development Corporation	EDC
France	Compagnie Fraçaise d'Assurance pour le Commerce Exterieur	COFACE
	Banque Francaise du Commerce Exterieur	BFCE
Germany	Treuarbeit Aktiengesellschaft	TREUARBEIT
India	Export Credit & Guarantee Corporation Limited	ECGC
Israel	The Israel Foreign Trade Risk Insurance Corporation Limited	IFTRIC
Japan	Export Insurance Division	EID
	Ministry of International Trade and Industry	MITI
Korea	The Export–Import Bank of Korea	EIBK
Netherlands	Nederlandsche Credietverzekering Maatschappij NV	NCM
New Zealand	Export Guarantee Office	EXGO
Norway	Garanti-Instituttet for Eksportkreditt	GIEK
South Africa	Credit Guarantee Insurance Corporation of Africa Limited	CGIC
Sweden	Exportkreditnamnden	EKN
Switzerland	Geschaftsstelle for die Exportrisikogarantie	GERG
United Kingdom	Exports Credits Guarantee Department	ECGD
United States	Export–Import Bank	EXIM

The joint venture

Joint ventures are often used in project finance. A definition of a joint venture, aka 'joint development company', is when two or more parties join to develop a project or series of projects. Joint ventures might include entities with different but complementary skills, e.g. a construction company, a project developer and a consultancy with the requisite legal and political skills to ensure project success in the host country (see political risks previously). Joint ventures can provide credit enhancement to the overall project risk profile, thereby rendering the loan facility more attractive (from a risk as well as pricing viewpoint) to the financial markets.

Guarantees

Guarantees are a key element of project finance. This is because of the huge amounts in question and the relatively limited balance sheet sizes of the project sponsors whose capitalization ratios would be adversely impacted. Guarantees enable promoters to move the financial risk of a project 'off the balance sheet' to one or more third parties. They thus provide a basis for shifting certain project finance risks to interested parties who do not want to take a direct financial commitment or provide funds to the project.

Guarantees therefore enable the sponsors to shift the liability off its balance sheet and at the same time achieve its goal of getting the project built. The nature and extent of guarantees can vary considerably and often depend on the nature of the project in question. The value of the guarantee moreover is directly a function of the guarantor's creditworthiness as well as the wording of the guarantee (e.g. whether it is a strong guarantee or a watered down 'letter of comfort'). Unless the guarantee is absolute and unconditional, it may not provide the requisite credit enhancement to comfort a lender that creditworthy support is in place.

It should be noted that guarantees can give lenders a false sense of security, since it is impossible to forecast whether they will be enforceable in a court of law. A guarantor seeking to avoid payment has many defences and a lender must obtain the necessary legal advice to ensure that the terms and conditions of the guarantee are drafted in a manner to preserve its rights against the guarantor.

There are various categories of guarantees:

- **Limited guarantees** Traditional guarantees represent direct, unconditional commitments by a guarantor to perform all the obligations of a third party. Limited guarantees as the name implies have some sort of limitation on them. Limited guarantees can provide credit enhancement without considerable impact on the guarantor's credit standing and financial statements. Limited guarantees include:
  - **construction phase guarantees** (guarantees that are effective only during the construction phase of a project);

- **claw-back guarantee** (ensures that the borrower returns cash distributions to the project company to the extent required by the project for such things as debt service, capital improvements and similar needs);
- **cash deficiency guarantee** (requires that the guarantor contribute additional capital to the project company should cash deficiencies arise);
- **completion guarantee** (designed to cover cost overrun risks by committing additional capital to the project company to the extent necessary to complete project construction).
- **Unlimited guarantees**   Unlimited guarantees are open-ended. While at first glance such guarantees seem the ultimate risk mitigation technique, in reality they can compromise the project since such a guarantee represents a tempting pool of cash for contractors, host governments, off-take purchasers and other project participants to tap. Such a guarantee could encourage contractors to generate cost overruns to the point that the project is no longer profitable. Such a guarantee – a credit enhancement device – would effectively have the perverse side effect of removing the ability to tightly control the project construction budget. It is important to consider therefore all possible ramifications of security and its side effects.
- **Indirect guarantees**   Indirect guarantees typically exist to ensure a steady stream of project revenues. Take-or-pay contracts, throughput contracts or long term unconditional transportation contracts, which were discussed earlier, are therefore effectively indirect guarantees. Such guarantees are indirect in accounting terms but are of crucial importance in a project financing.
- **Implied guarantees**   An implied guarantee is a way of assuring the lender that the 'guarantor' will provide 'necessary support' to the project. Implied guarantees are not legally binding and, as such, do not require financial statement reporting. Implied guarantees should not be confused with *comfort letters*. These are letters in which the 'guarantor' addresses a risk concern of the lender (e.g. an expression of an intent not to sell the project company or change its name). Since corporate objectives and boards change with the weather, such letters can rapidly run counter to strategies yet to be defined. Since comfort letters are not guarantees, it is therefore safe to say that they constitute nothing more than window dressing since they are not enforceable in a court of law.

- **Contingent guarantees** are guarantees contingent on an event, or events happening (e.g. the failure of other interested parties to the transaction to fulfil their commitments to pay after 'reasonable efforts' – which is not easy to define in court– by a lender to enforce performance or collection of same). Contingent guarantees may provide sufficient support to 'credit enhance' the facility commensurate with market demand.
- **Government assurances**   Projects in the national interest may warrant the banks requiring the government to extend a guarantee. For example, the lender will seek assurances from the state body that they will not take actions that may adversely affect the project (e.g. tariffs, tax, duty and excise, etc.). Governmental support may be provided via comfort letters, support agreements or loan agreements. Such governmental commitments may require approval by local legislative bodies (e.g. in Russia loans with governmental guarantee on amounts above US$100 million require ratification from the State Duma).
- **Sovereign guarantees**   In a sovereign guarantee, the host government guarantees to the project company that if certain events do or do not occur, the government will compensate the project company. This is usually the case when the borrower is of a weak creditworthiness but the project is deemed to be in the national interest (typically infrastructural). The scope of a sovereign guarantee depends on the unique risks of a project.

Security

Creating appropriate security structures is so important that it can often necessitate changes in how a project is structured. Since typically the lenders will have no recourse to assets of the project company (other than the project assets) and will look primarily to the cash flow generated by the project to repay loans to the project company, it is therefore essential that lenders ensure that valid and effective security interests are taken over all the project assets. Moreover, it is essential that lenders fully understand the local legal system and how enforcement of security may not be as satisfactory as that in their own home systems. If problems do arise with the project and the lenders are forced to pursue their security interests then, in the absence of any shareholder guarantees or other tangible support, the enforcing of their security over the project assets will be the only opportunity for the lenders to recover their loans.

Reasons for taking security

The main reason for taking security is to ensure that the lenders are able to sell the asset in question on any enforcement of their security. In most jurisdictions, realizing security on moveable assets will not pose insurmountable problems, although in some jurisdictions this can be an expensive and time-consuming exercise. With most projects, however, the ability to sell the project assets is not the prime motivation for taking security. The prime motivators are:

■ **The security package is a defensive mechanism** designed both to prevent other (possibly unsecured) creditors taking security over the assets which they have financed and to prevent other creditors trying to attach those assets or take other enforcement action in respect of them. If the lenders cannot sell the project assets and repay themselves out of the proceeds, then they certainly do not want any other creditors interfering with those assets in any way. Usually, the project lenders will structure the facility to ensure that there are no significant creditors other than those within the project.

■ **The security package is a control mechanism** to enable the lenders to control the destiny of the project should things start to go wrong. The lenders will hope that their security interests will provide sufficient leverage to wrest control from the project company, enabling them to control the project directly (e.g. complete the project (if necessary) and operate it in order to generate the cash flows needed to repay themselves). However, the ability of the lenders to be able to achieve this aim will depend to a large extent on the jurisdiction in which the principal project assets are located.

Security over specific tangible assets

In many projects there will be some specific tangible assets which can be separated from the project used by the banks for security. It is unlikely, however, that the value of such assets in a liquidation fetch a value sufficient to cover the overall debts. Such assets would include the tangible assets used in the facilities, the land, buildings and other fixtures of the project company, licenses or other operating permits (provided they are transferable), technology and process licences, and any other assets such as the goods being produced by the project, and other rights under the underlying project.

Negative pledge

A negative pledge is a contractual commitment on the part of the borrower not to create encumbrances over its assets in favour of any third party. This however may not suffice to protect the lender's position because if the borrower were to create security in favour of a third party (in contravention of the negative pledge), it is quite likely that the security would in most jurisdictions be regarded as valid. Therefore, while the borrower might be liable for having breached its contractual obligations, this will provide little comfort to the lender if it is relying on the project assets as a source of repayment. It is possible that if the third party knew of the existence of the negative pledge, that the lender might be able to challenge the validity of any security created in breach of it, however, the onus of proof will lie with the lending bank, which may be unpleasantly surprised at the results yielded by the country's legal system.

Security trusts

Project financings often rely on security trustees to process project revenues. Security trusts represent a convenient way of taking and holding security in those jurisdictions where the concept of a trust is recognized. Security trusts offer two advantages:

- they facilitate the trading of loans by the lenders without any danger of releasing security; and
- they remove the insolvency risk of an agent or other third party holding the security.

Table 2.2 Taking security checklist

1 Which assets does the borrower own?
   Which assets does it merely has a right to use (e.g. under a licence)?

2 Can security can be created over user rights as well as ownership rights?

3 Over what project assets can a fixed security be created?

4 Are any floating charges are possible?

5 Can security be created over assets not in existence at the time of creation of the charge?

6 Can security over moveable assets be created without physical transfer of those assets to the mortgagee or pledgee?

7 What degree of control must the chargee exercise over the assets to constitute a fixed, as opposed to floating, charge?

8 Are there any restrictions on foreigners taking security, especially overland?

9 Which creditors will, by law, be preferred over a secured creditor?

10 Can third parties (including joint ventures under terms of pre-emption or similar rights in underlying documents) or a liquidator interfere with the granting of security or its enforcement?

11 Can the lenders, when a default occurs, appoint a receiver over the assets?

12 Can the banks be held responsible for the receiver's actions or can the receiver be appointed as agent for the borrower?

13 Can the lenders, upon enforcement, control the sale of the assets or must there be a court sale or public auction?

14 Is it necessary to obtain the third party's consent when enforcing security over claims against third parties (e.g. debts, receivables, shares, bonds, notes)?

15 What formalities need to be complied with to perfect security-notarizations, registrations, filings and stamp duties?

16 Can the security be held by an agent or trustee for a group of creditors whose members might change from time to time (e.g. through transfer of their participation in the facility to another bank)?

In those jurisdictions where trusts are not recognized, it may still be possible for one of the banks to act as security agent on behalf of the other lenders, although the insolvency of the security agent becomes a risk for the lenders.

Formalities

Whatever security is taken, it will need to satisfy the security formalities in the relevant jurisdiction. Security will typically be governed by English or New York law. However, security over the assets situated in the project company's jurisdiction, and often any concession agreement or licence, will generally be governed by local law. It is therefore essential that the lenders be aware of the formalities relating to the jurisdiction in question, and ensure that the security is perfected in accordance with local laws if it to be enforceable. Such formalities may be relevant both at the time the security is taken and also at the time of enforcement.

Insurance issues

Role of project insurance

Insurance is an aspect of project finance which concerns the project sponsors and the lenders equally. Lenders view insurance as an integral and key element of their overall security package for a project, especially in the event of a major casualty or disaster. It is, therefore essential to ensure that an appropriate insurance structure be in place for a project financing.

The bank will require an insurance policy which ensures that the project is restored to operability should an accident or force majeure cause contractual failure. Lenders may also require insurance against business interruption. This will result in a cash transfer to the lenders, who can then decide whether to permit the insurance proceeds to be used to rebuild the damaged assets or whether to apply the insurance monies towards the debt.

Types of insurance

There are several types of insurance policies available to cover risks in project financings. Some of these are described below. Note that not all types are appropriate since legislation changes from country to country.

- **Contractor's all risks**   Project finance contractors are typically required to obtain property damage insurance such as 'all risk' builder's risk insurance to pay for direct loss or damage occurring to the work during construction.

■ **Advanced loss of revenue**   Advanced loss of revenue insurance protects against the potential loss of revenue arising from delays following an insured loss or damage during the construction period.

■ **Marine cargo**   Marine cargo insurance is available to provide protection against loss or damage caused to equipment and materials during transit from the shipper to the project site.

■ **Marine advanced loss of revenue**   Marine advanced loss of revenue provides insurance protection against the financial consequences for loss of revenue as a result of a delay following an insured loss or damage.

■ **Operator's all risks**   Operator's all risks provides protection against loss or damage, however caused, occurring after commercial operation (including coverage on equipment being overhauled or repaired off the site).

■ **Operator's loss of revenue**   Operator's loss of revenue coverage protects against lost revenue arising from physical loss or damage after completion of the project.

■ **Third party liability**   Third party liability coverage provides protection against damage and losses attributable to legal liability for bodily injury and property damage.

■ **Exchange rate fluctuations**   This is a particular concern where there is a decision not to rebuild a project after a casualty. If the exchange of insurance proceeds can be approved in advance, then this should be done. Alternatively, it may be prudent to require the local insurer to re-insure the risk off-shore, and then have the proceeds payable under the re-insurance contract assigned to the project company for payment should a loss occur.

■ **Export financing requirements**   Export credit agencies may require the project to obtain insurance from companies in the export bank's home country.

■ **Warranty**   Warranties extend protection to the project after the project is completed. Most are limited to obligations to repair or replace the defective construction or equipment. Warranties are sometimes considered 'quasi-insurance' because they may provide compensation for defects not covered by insurance.

Scope of cover

Cover will vary between the construction and operating phases of a project. Typically, insurance cover for each phase is set out below:

Construction phase:	Operating phase:
Physical damage to project facilities	Insurance against physical damage to project facilities
Physical damage to other assets	Insurance against physical damage to other assets
Transit insurance, e.g. parts in transit	Transit insurance covering the periods until point of sale
Employers, workmen's compensation and third party liability insurance	Employers' and workmen's compensation
Environmental liability insurance	Environmental liability insurance
Delay in start-up insurance	Business interruption or loss of profits insurance

Problem areas

It is impossible to predict all problem areas, but the following checklist identifies some of the principal concerns from a lender's perspective.

- The policy may be cancelled, either in accordance with its terms by agreement between the insured and the insurers, or by the brokers for non-payment of premiums.
- The policy may expire and not be renewed.
- The policy may be changed so as adversely to affect the cover provided – for example, the scope of the policy may be narrowed, policy limits may be reduced or deductibles may be increased (deductibles are, of course, a form of self-insurance).
- The loss may be caused by a peril which was not insured, and so (for example) a policy which covers political risks such as war, revolution and insurrection should be checked further to ensure that it also covers politically motivated violent acts such as terrorism or sabotage.

- The policy may be avoided by the insurers on the grounds of breach of warranty by the insured.
- The insured may not make any (or any timely) claim for indemnity under the policy.
- The insurers may be insolvent and unable to pay a claim.
- The claim may be paid by the insurers to the brokers but somehow lost in the broker's insolvency.
- The broker may assert a lien (i.e. a special proprietary claim) against any unpaid premiums which are due from the insured.
- A claim may be paid to the insured by the brokers but somehow lost in the borrower's insolvency.
- The occurrence of any or a combination of these events could result in the insurance moneys not being received by the lenders, as expected, with the result that the lenders could find themselves unsecured for all or part of the project loan.

Performance and payment bonds

- **Bid bonds** are used typically by a host government that desires to ensure that the project sponsor that wins a bid for an infrastructure facility actually proceeds with the project.
- **Performance bonds** are issued by a surety to a project company, and is usually assigned to the project lender as part of the project collateral.
- **Payment bonds** are callable if the contractor fails to pay some amount that is due under the terms of the construction contract.
- **Retention money bonds.** Contractors sometimes provide retention money bonds to the project company as security for project completion. The contractor can then receive and use the money that would otherwise be retained. If construction is not completed, the project company can apply the contingency amount covered by the bond for project completion.

Reinsurance

Sometimes use is made of reinsurers. This is usually because the principal insurer does not have the capacity to absorb the full risk insured against.

Chapter 3

Evaluating the project

The offering memorandum

As a first step in the syndications sales cycle, the agent bank together with the project sponsors will prepare an offering memorandum (also known as an information memorandum). This occurs in the early phases of the loan syndication, as depicted in the syndication timeline shown in Figure 3.1.

Here, we look at the information memorandum as a sales/information tool. Most potential participants in a syndicated loan are expected to exercise prudent credit judgement by undertaking their own credit analysis. The process of credit analysis does not concern us here, we only note that there is a standard approach to assessing lending risks which typically includes obtaining information such as certificates of incorporation, authorized signatories, annual reports, auditor's certificates, etc. In the case of syndicated loans, the agent typically obtains this information from the borrower.

In any project finance transaction there are elements that fall outside the scope of traditional frameworks and checklists. This is particularly the case in transactions of a unique nature such as aircraft leasing or project financing. This could include information to supplement the traditional sources of credit information such as maps of the oil fields in question, estimated demand for oil, forecasted oil prices and various tables quantifying this. In other words, information relating to the specifics of the project being financed as opposed to the borrower's financial condition.

The purpose of the memorandum is to explain the project to potential lenders, including topics such as: experience of the project sponsors;

SYNDICATIONS TIMETABLE – FROM MANDATE TO DRAWDOWN

Phase	Week 1	Week 2	Week 3	Week 4	Week 5	Week 6	Week 7	Week 8
Mandate awarded	■							
Prepare first draft of facility agreement with legal counsel	■							
Prepare information memorandum	■	■						
Allocate participations and send invitations to banks		■						
Review/refine first draft of facility agreement		■						
Second draft of facility agreement from counsel		■						
Send invitations and letters of confidentiality to banks			■					
Send information memorandum and loan documents to banks			■					
Wait for banks to obtain individual credit approvals			■	■	■			
Negotiate facility agreement from borrower				■				
Sign draft facility agreement with borrower					■			
Wait for banks to review facility agreement						■		
Collect loan administration details						■	■	
Make final allocations							■	
Arrange signing ceremony							■	
Signing closing								■
Transfer syndications file to facility agent								■
Satisfy conditions precedent								■
DRAWDOWN								■

Figure 3.1 Syndications timetable

the identity and experience of the project participants (contractor, operator, suppliers and off-take purchasers); information on the host government; summaries of the project contracts; project risks, and how the risks are addressed; proposed financing terms; the construction budget; financial projections; and financial information about the project sponsors and other project participants. The purpose of the memorandum is to sell the loan – to help 'the participating banks reach a credit decision, especially small banks that do not have seasoned credit analysts'.

Every professionally produced information memorandum has a disclaimer, or, more discreetly, 'important notice' as its first item. This disclaimer typically states with solemnity that 'the document is not intended to provide the sole basis for any credit or other evaluation, is meant to inform, and is not a recommendation to buy'. This seems to suggest that no value can be placed on its content.

To put matters in perspective, the 'information memorandum' in effect is a marketing document, despite the presence of these disclaimers. The presence of these disclaimers can be traced back to lawsuits where certain lenders sued an arranger for alleged misrepresentation of the borrower's financial condition as depicted in the information memorandum. The case was settled out of court with the agent bank repaying each of the lenders in full. Disclaimers have since been incorporated as standard operating procedure. Information memoranda nevertheless do not absolve the participating bank of undertaking its own independent analysis and exercising prudent credit judgement.

Legislation relating to information memoranda

Typically, information memoranda are released to potential lenders following the signing of a confidentiality agreement and letter of authority from the borrower authorizing the agent to release the information memorandum.

The information memorandum is a formal and confidential document prepared by the agent bank in conjunction with the borrower. The arranger uses information provided by the borrower plus other official and unofficial sources, and the memorandum should ideally address all the principal credit issues relating to the borrower and more specifically the project being financed. The information memorandum is the most important document in the syndications process since it acts as a marketing tool as well as a source of information.

Information memoranda are typically prepared by the agent and borrower, and a disclaimer, usually in block letters on the cover, will state that the circular is 'for information purposes only' and 'not a recommendation to participate'. This is a document fraught with dangers for the lead bank in terms of the potential liabilities flowing from it and it is ironic that many lead banks only rarely take legal advice when preparing it.

There are two major sources of liability in relation to the soliciting of syndicate members by way of the information memorandum:

- The first is any relevant prospectus legislation in the countries in which it is distributed (e.g. the Companies Act 1985 and the Financial Services Act 1986).
- The second is misrepresentation should the statements in the information memorandum be incorrect or incomplete.

It is strongly recommended that agent banks preparing information memoranda seek the proper legal counsel in order to ensure that they are not exposing themselves legally by preparing and furnishing such a document.

It should be noted that while the arranging bank can expose itself legally by preparing and distributing an information memorandum, the arranger takes no responsibility for the completeness or accuracy of the information provided in the memorandum, and that providing an information memorandum does not disengage participating banks from the responsibility of undertaking their own independent analysis. It is up to the banks to evaluate the economic and financial aspects of a transaction before entering into a commitment.

Many jurisdictions have introduced legislation regulating prospectuses inviting public subscription for securities. Generally it may be said that if the information memorandum is to be within the legislation then:

■ It may have to contain prescribed information.
■ It may have to be registered (e.g. with a securities commission, a registrar of companies, or some other authority).
■ The liabilities for misrepresentation may be more onerous.

Almost always, however, the information memorandum will fall within an exemption depending upon the circumstances. The principal ones are:

■ The syndication constitutes a private offering and not a public invitation.
■ The information memorandum is issued only to sophisticated 'investors' who can look after themselves.
■ The borrower is a government or government body.
■ The participations do not constitute 'securities' or 'debentures' within the relevant legislation.
■ The information memorandum is issued only to foreign residents of foreign nationals.

However, we need to consider UK legislation in greater detail because one cannot assume that the syndication will benefit from an exception. The Companies Act 1985/New Legislation 1995, has this to say about the contents of the information memorandum:

> *The Companies Act 1985 requires the inclusion of specified information in a prospectus or circular offering to the public, for subscription or purchase, debentures of a company, whether domestic or foreign. The Act applies to any person who issues such a prospectus or circular in the UK regardless of his nationality.*

As far as the information memorandum is concerned, the important words are 'debentures' and 'public'. Thus, if there is no 'debenture' (i.e. a document evidencing a debt), the information memorandum will escape and if the information memorandum is not distributed to the 'public', it will escape. Moreover, if the borrower is a foreign company, then an information memorandum issued to professional dealers in securities will also be exempt.

The relevant provisions of the 1985 Act are to be superseded by new legislation from the Council of the European Communities numbered 89/298/EEC.

The typical information memorandum includes:

- **Disclaimer**   It is important that it be clearly and prominently displayed.
- **Authority letter**   Here the borrower authorizes release of the information memorandum to the syndicate.
- **Project overview**   A brief description of the proposed project is included first in the memorandum. The overview includes the type of project, background on the host country, the status of development and other significant information.
- **Borrower**   The description of the borrower explains the form of organization (corporation, partnership, limited liability company) and place of organization of the borrower. It includes the ownership structure of the borrower.
- **Project sponsors**   The identity, role and involvement of the project sponsors in the project is included. Summary financial information about the sponsors is also given. This section also specifies the management structure of the project company.
- **Debt amount/uses of proceeds**   How much debt the project will need is described generally in this section. Also included is the currency in which the loan is to be made and repaid. The manner in which loan proceeds will be used is an important part of the memorandum.
- **Sources of debt and equity**   The total construction budget and working capital needs of the project, including start-up pre-operation costs, are outlined in this section. Also, the sources of the funds needed for the project are explained, including debt and equity.
- **Collateral**   This discussion includes the identity of collateral, whether the collateral is junior in lien priority to other debt, and any special collateral considerations.
- **Equity terms**   The terms of the equity are more completely described in this section. Included are explanations of the type of equity investments;

when the equity will be contributed; how the equity will be funded, whether the commitment is absolute or subject to conditions, and if conditional, why it is conditional.

- **Cost overruns** The offering memorandum may set forth an explanation of how any cost overruns will be funded.
- **Sponsor guarantee/credit enhancement** Any other guarantees or credit enhancement that the project sponsors will provide are also described.
- **Debt amortization** This section describes the proposed debt repayment terms, including amortization schedules and dates for repayment of interest and principal. Mechanical elements such as minimum amounts of prepayments, advance notice of prepayments, may also be described (but are governed by the loan agreement).
- **Commitment, drawdown and cancellation of commitment** The mechanical provisions are typically included, although they are generally identical boilerplate clauses in standard loan contracts. These include minimum drawdown amounts, and timing and notice of drawdowns.
- **Interest rate** Typical interest rate options include a bank's prime (or reference) rate, being the rate typically offered to its best customers, LIBOR (London Interbank Offered Rate), Cayman (rates of banks with respect to Cayman Island branches), and HIBOR (Hong Kong Interbank Offered Rate). Rates can, of course, also be fixed.
- **Fees** The fees offered to the lenders, including structuring fees, closing fees, underwriting fees and commitment fees, are described. Amounts are usually left blank and resolved during negotiations.
- **Governing law** In this section the choice of law to govern the loan documents is listed. It is sometimes the law of the host country. However, that is not so in financings in developing countries, unless lenders in the host country provide all debt.
- **Lawyers, advisers and consultants** This section will identify the lawyers, advisers and consultants involved in the project; often a budget for legal fees is requested.

Information memorandum issues

Before any project can be 'sold' to commercial lenders, its feasibility – technical and economic – must be presented in a convincing and authoritative manner. This is done via the preparation of the information memorandum which will cite opinions from technical experts, financial and legal advisers and a review of the project.

The purpose of the information memorandum is to sell the deal to other banks, and it does this by selectively providing technical, economic, contractual, governmental and market information on the proposed project This report is used by the project sponsor to generate interest with potential lenders, government officials and potential equity investors.

In order to maximize the potential of generating interest different reports might be prepared for each of these audiences, as one would prepare different CVs for different employers. These information memoranda effectively pre-prepare the analytical grunt work for potential providers of capital. The information memorandum will include several specific sections.

- **General description** The feasibility study generally begins with an overview description of the project. The location is specified, usually including a map of the project site, and other ancillary details anyone with a computer can extract from the World Wide Web. The more statistical information one can compile on the country and economy, preferably from official sources such as the OECD, the more authoritative the feasibility study appears. Statistical data can come from sources such as rating agencies, the OECD, and the US Department of Commerce, which cover esoteria such as topography, weather, drainage, major landmarks, population density, access to transportation and housing, water and wastewater treatment facilities and other data. Data that threatens to obfuscate the analysis is conveniently ignored so that it does not interfere with the marketing of the transaction.
- **Project sponsors and project company** Ownership interests in the project company are specified in detail, as is management control. This includes the standard corporate-produced prose on the background and experience of the project sponsors. (The feasibility study will be selective in quoting various successful previous projects. Past embarrassments do not figure in this marketing exercise; the whole point is to impress potential investors with the vast and omniscient experience of the project sponsors, and their immaculate track record.)

■ **Project participants** Participants such as the contractor, operator, fuel supplier, off-take purchaser, local and central governments etc. are obviously described in flattering terms. In addition, linkage of the participants to previous projects, stressing anything that is positive and ostensibly relevant, is made. Biographies, financial information, credit ratings and anything likely to impress investors is incorporated into the report. To the extent detailed financial information about the participants is available, such as securities filings, this information is also included, but no analytical judgements are offered since doing so might be construed as a recommendation to participate, which could be an awkward accusation to deal with should the deal experience difficulties.

■ **Technical information** The technical information section of the feasibility study provides an overview description of the proposed project and also explains the technology and processes that will be used. Since banks save money by firing analysts, this technical information is designed to impress by volume and depth, as opposed to providing practical information for a decision. Moreover, most bankers are incapable of understanding this technical information, so the exercise is basically designed to reassure bank officers and credit committees and satisfy the legal requirements that the transaction was properly analysed. Accordingly, the more exhaustive and complete the information, the more impressive. The fact that much of this information may be have no direct cause and effect linkage is irrelevant, because the whole exercise is designed to impress, not inform, readers who are technically deficient.

One publication cites on its list of information esoteria such as fuel sources (try predicting the price of oil in three years' time); infrastructure transportation; utilities (availability); water (sources, quality, treatment, transportation); roads and railways, ports and docks (need, type); raw materials (sources and supply); local labour (availability and skills); subcontractors (availability, qualifications); construction and operation labour (training, housing needs); spare parts (availability, delivery time, on-site supply needs); and residue and other waste disposal (sites, transportation, liability). It is doubtful MI5 or the CIA, let alone a bank, could realistically provide reliable information on the above. Lengthy discussions which are maddeningly unspecific may be included in the documentation. Indeed, reading the technical elements of an information memorandum 10 years later may reveal the document to be nothing more than an exercise in creative writing.

■ **Economic information**   Despite the fact that economists and governments cannot plan economic policy since they are typically at the service of ideologues, bankers want economic information in the feasibility study, so this information is included. Explanations of economic information relating to the construction, operating and financing expenses for the proposed project and an estimate of the investment return for the project sponsor will feature. These projections usually bear no link to reality (e.g. Eurotunnel, or some oil companies' estimated oil reserves), but that is not the point. The essential matter is to come up with a forecast that can be passed through a credit committee, so that the deal can be clinched.

■ **Contracts**   The information memorandum will include an analysis of the documentation and credit enhancement structure. Any particularities relating to the legal framework in the host country will be noted, typically via expert legal opinions. Agreements can include the development agreement, partnership agreement or joint venture agreement; the project management agreement; the construction contract; the operating agreement; any site leases or other real property contracts; fuel and raw material supply agreements; output sale agreements; waste disposal agreements; host country agreements; etc. Beyond general information about these contracts, each description generally contains schedules for negotiating the contracts, details on current negotiations, major issues not yet agreed upon and other similar details.

■ **Project schedule**   The time schedule for the development, construction and initial operation of the project should be included, with all important milestones noted. This includes the obtaining of relevant government approvals and permits.

■ **Government**   The host government is described in the study, together with information about the likelihood of its support for the project. This often is a meaningless PR exercise because unpleasant realities such as rigged elections, media censorship, torture, cronyism, or corrupt government officials siphoning off funds from similar projects into overseas bank accounts or asking for cash commissions will be omitted since this would offend the relevant government and be counterproductive

to the project. Therefore, such analysis typically is of a bland, inoffen-
sive and uninformative nature included for sake of formality as
opposed to any meaningful analysis. It is therefore up to the bankers to
undertake their own independent research into underlying realities.

■ **Market**　Naturally it is important to identify and quantify the market
demand for the goods or services provided by the proposed project.
Accordingly, analysis of the good and market information typically
includes descriptions of possible users of the project's production and
the financial viability of these uses. This adopts the classic financial
analysis techniques of identifying risks such as Michael Porter's Risk
Assessment model. Analysis will typically focus on comparing the cost
of purchasing the off-take from the proposed project versus the costs
from alternative, existing sources. Particular focus will be on governmental policies for the economy; sector organization and analysis, or
plans for privatisation of government-owned companies in the same
sector; and industry trends that might affect the market for the project's output. Likewise, if the output will be exported, analysis will
focus on the specific geographic regions in which sales are feasible,

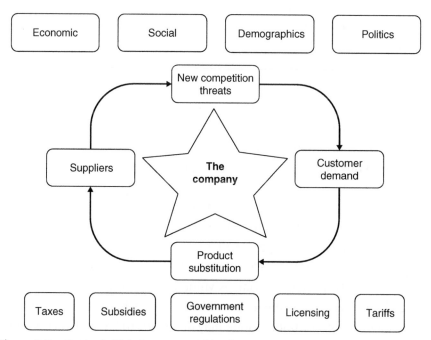

Figure 3.2　Porter's Risk Assessment Matrix

and legal, regulatory and financial constraints to export and import of the output.

- **Independent engineer** Since projects are technically complex endeavours, it is necessary to have specialists monitor the project to ensure that funds are not being skimmed off (for example, selling construction materials in the local bazaar), or that the project construction meets the technical criteria (e.g. proper safety, fireproofing, etc. is implemented). This is to avoid embarrassing incidents as well as the legal liability arising from events such as the collapse of the roof of the Charles de Gaulle Airport Terminal 2 in Paris or the oscillating Millennium Bridge in London. Also, success of the project depends on its ability to generate adequate cash flow to pay operating costs, service debt and generate equity return. Typically, these 'independent engineers' are specialists in a particular industry, and have large amounts of reports prepared on similar topics for past deals. The 'analysis' basically consists in recycling some past review of a similar project and updating it for the project in question. Obviously, the 'independent engineer' will conclude that the project is feasible (since to do otherwise would sink the deal and not result in future consulting business for the 'independent engineer'). The 'independent engineer's' report typically covers: engineering and design; construction; project start-up; operation and maintenance; input supply; off-take production; and financial projections. The report may also include analysis of local operating conditions; previous design vulnerabilities at similar projects; new technologies; the construction schedule and contractor incentives for timely project completion; operating budget contingencies; preventive maintenance plans; and suitability of assumptions in the financial projections.

- **Access to raw materials** If the project is dependent upon access to raw materials, the report will address these issues. For example, if a government grants a concession for the development of a mine, the project will also need access to domestic supplies for other strategic raw materials, such as oil or gas. In these cases, the government may agree to make the raw materials available to the project at a certain price. If access to critical raw materials is vulnerable, guarantees or insurance should be included wherever possible. In cases where access is not controlled by the government, there may be means to facilitate access such as by having the government waive or reduce the tariffs for such items.

- **Obtaining operating licences and permits**   Operating licences and permits constitute the most valuable property of the project in the initial stage. Their availability is evidenced by documents of transfer signed by the highest level official in the government who is authorized to grant such licences and permits. In many countries, obtaining such permits is facilitated by the payment of cash commissions. It is often difficult to obtain receipts for the payment of such cash commissions. It is essential that these permits be transferable in order to maintain the on-sale value of the project. If the licences and permits are not transferable, then the owners of the project have in effect no market value for their assets (except perhaps for the salvage value of the equipment and raw materials). The availability and transferability issues will need to be specifically addressed in the bankable proposal and backed up by transfer of ownership documentation signed by the original owner.
- **Project profitability**   The projection of costs and returns dictates the profitability and cash flow of the project. Financial projections should therefore factor in variables such as interest rates, exchange rates, inflation, taxes, delays and other contingencies. For a full description of the pro forma financial projections required for a project, one should use a developed spreadsheet model along the lines of the simplified model exhibited below in this chapter (see pp. 102–103).
- **Environmental legislation**   Environmental compliance is becoming an increasingly important issue. It is essential therefore that the project comply with these directives. Whatever the requirements, the project owner needs to assure the bank that all such requirements will be fulfilled. Likewise, the bank may require, as a condition precedent, that the loan agreement becomes binding only after the successful completion of all the necessary environmental requirements. It is essential therefore that one obtains a legal opinion on the environmental legislation and requirements in effect in the host country.
- **Foreign exchange risk**   Many countries still have currencies that are not freely convertible. This may pose a problem to the project's viability. For large projects, it may be necessary to have the government lift foreign exchange controls. For large projects, this may be necessary in order for the project to have any chance of success. However, for smaller projects this might not be a politically viable solution. In such cases, alternative

mechanisms may be necessary, such as barter agreements (oil for goods). Foreign exchange risk should not be underestimated since in the case of major currency movements, this can render dollar denominated projects excessively expensive to service with local currency revenues.

- **Project and country risk insurance**   Insurance against project risks is critically important for the initiation of the project and insurance policies should therefore be made part of the bankable proposal since, without it, if the project is unable to pay back the loan, it may have to be written off as a complete loss. Moreover, given the currency crises witnessed during the 1990s, it appears that insurance against country risks would also be necessary in order to enable lenders to consider assuming the risks of a major project financing.
- **Financial appraisal of the project**   Depending on who you are, there are several ways to evaluate whether a project is financially viable. For example, while international financial institutions prefer to use a discounted cash flow (DCF) model, companies are likely to use simple payback methods to calculate the costs and benefits of small-sized projects with short term completion horizons (within one to three years). Projects with longer payback periods however will typically rely on the DCF model.
- **Investment appraisal**   The main method of calculating the viability of the project is the net present value (NPV) method of calculation. Project NPV of the investment project should be subjected to base case and sensitivity analysis accounting for different scenarios. There are four steps in calculating the value of a capital investment:
  - forecast the project's incremental (after-tax) cash flows;
  - assess the project's risk;
  - estimate the opportunity cost of capital (the expected rate of return offered to investors versus that of equivalent-risk investments traded in the capital markets);
  - calculate NPV using the discounted cash flow formula.
- **Calculating project costs**   The first step in assessing the financial viability of a project finance proposal is to determine all the costs of the project. These can be categorized as follows:
  - **Capital costs and depreciation of the project**   Capital costs include land, building, facilities, equipment and machinery, which are bought and paid for in one year and reside in the business for subsequent

years. The capital costs of the project will be accounted as an asset and depreciated over subsequent years.

■ **Operating costs**   These include direct costs of raw materials, labour and energy costs other than fuels and maintenance. Indirect costs such as storage, rates and rent, insurance and handling also apply. There are further general overhead costs due to administration and distribution activities. These should be well detailed.

■ **Fixed *vs.* variable costs**   Fixed costs are just that – costs that do not change with the output of the plant. These include: local tax, rent, rates, insurance, space heating and lighting. Variable costs vary in function of the output of the project, e.g. raw materials, manufacturing energy, fuel, equipment maintenance, packaging, labour, etc.

Cash flow

Cash flow represents the actual difference between money coming in and money going out of the investment project (Figure 3.3). Cash flows should

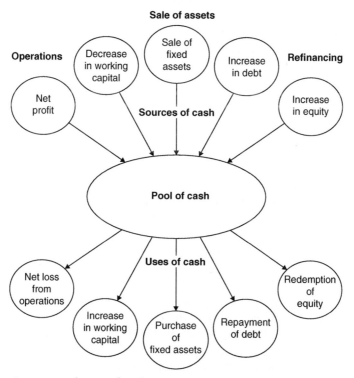

Figure 3.3   Sources and uses of cash

(£000s)	2000	2001	2002	2003	2004	2005	2006	2007
Gross revenues	0	0	360	1124	1304	1236	1150	712
Capital expenditures	540	780	80	0	0	0	0	0
Operating costs	0	0	124	132	148	164	180	196
Taxes	0	0	0	0	376	564	528	432
Cash flow before debt service	**540**	**790**	**156**	**992**	**780**	**508**	**442**	**84**
Drawdowns	460	664	0	0	0	0	0	0
Debt repayments	0	0	0	308	310	308	308	0
Interest payment	0	0	124	124	92	62	30	0
Cash flow to sponsor	**80**	**116**	**32**	**560**	**378**	**138**	**104**	**84**
Debt amortization								
Starting debt balance	0	480	1234	1234	926	618	308	0
Drawdowns	460	664	0	0	0	0	0	0
Principal repayment	0	0	0	308	310	308	308	0
Interest rolled over	20	90	0	0	0	0	0	0
Ending loan balance	480	1234	1234	926	616	308	0	0

Figure 3.4 Simplified project finance cash flow

Summary of cash flow model:
Gross revenue: The forecast level of income to as calculated by the project company (assumptions should be tested)

Capital expenditures
Operating costs: The capital costs and operating costs are estimates of what it will cost to build and run the project. Capital costs only apply during the building of the project. Operating costs, due to production increases and inflation increase steadily during the entire life of the project

Taxes: Taxes are calculated in function of any agreements and the tax environment in the country in question. It is important to explain how the tax rate is being calculated

Cash flow pre-debt service: This is line 1 minus lines 2, 3 and 4. This shows how much cash flow the company has before paying financing costs. Bankers typically like this cash flow figure to be at least 150% of financing costs

Drawdowns: This scenario assumes that 85% of the capital costs are financed by the banks in the first two years. Capital costs incurred in year 2 are financed from the project cash flows in year 1 of production

Debt (loan) repayment: The loan repayment schedule features 4 equal yearly instalments starting in year 3. Repayment schedules are the result of cash flow projections, project dynamics and negotiation and can vary considerably (see Table 3.1)

Interest repayment: The projections assume an interest rate of 10% per annum on the loan amount outstanding at the start of year 3. There is no interest in years 1 and 2 since no revenue is being generated and interest is therefore capitalized

Table 3.1   Loan repayment schedules

	1	2	3	4	5	6	7	8	Total
Straight line	125	125	125	125	125	125	125	125	1000
Variable	50	150	150	250	100	50	50	200	1000
Balloon	50	50	50	50	50	50	50	650	1000
Bullet	0	0	0	0	0	0	0	1000	1000

not be confused with accounting profits and losses. Consequently, the P/L statement needs to be adjusted in order to transform the investment project's (income statement) earnings into the project's cash flows. For example, depreciation charges have to be added as they do not correspond to a cash outflow at all, increases in assets (account receivables and inventories and borrowings) will have to be deducted and increases in liabilities (account payables, bank debt, equity) added back.

Financial ratios

Financial ratio analysis can take two forms:

- Historical ratio analysis: this looks at the company's performance over time.
- Peer group analysis: this compares the company's performance to other similar companies in similar industry sectors.

Figure 3.4   *(continued)*

Cash flow to sponsor: This is negative during the first two years because the sponsors are committing funds to the project. After year 2 the project produces a positive cash flow to the sponsors after debt service

Debt amortization
Starting loan balance: This shows the outstanding of the loan at the beginning of the year

Drawdowns

Principal repayment

Loan rolled over

End loan balance: This shows the outstanding of the loan at the end of the year

General financial ratios for various industries are published by the Risk Management Association (ex Robert Morris Associates), Dun & Bradstreet, BVD-Amadeus and various other credit agencies and trade associations.

Financial ratios can be divided into four types pertaining to:

- liquidity
- debt
- profitability
- covering ratios.

The first two types are ratios computed from the balance sheet; the last two are ratios computed from the income statement and, sometimes, from both the income statement and the balance sheet.

The table 3.2 depicts the main financial ratio categories for corporates.

We discuss certain ratios which are particularly relevant in project finance analysis, which looks to future cash flows as opposed to classic balance sheet ratios.

Liquidity ratios

Liquidity ratios are used to judge a firm's ability to meet short term obligations. The main ratio to measure liquidity is the current ratio.

$$\frac{\text{Current assets}}{\text{Current liabilities}}$$

The higher the ratio, the greater the ability of the firm to pay its bills. However, the ratio does not take into account the liquidity of the individual components of the current assets, such as inventory, receivables (stock, work in progress, debtors) etc.

Table 3.2 Financial ratio categories

Return On Equity	= net income before dividends/total net worth
Profitability	= net income before dividends/net sales
Efficiency	= net sales/total assets
Capital Structure	= total assets/total net worth

Efficiency Ratios

Debtors Days	= trade debtors/net sales × 365
Total Stocks Days	= raw materials + work in progress + finished goods/cost of goods sold × 365
Raw Materials Days	= raw materials/cost of goods sold × 365
Work In Progress Days	= work in progress/cost of goods sold × 365
Finished Goods Days	= finished goods/cost of goods sold × 365
Creditors Days	= trade creditors/cost of goods sold × 365
Accruals Days	= accruals/cost of goods sold × 365
Net Plant Turnover	= net sales/net fixed assets
Working Investment/Sales	= [(trade debtors + stocks) − (trade creditors + accruals)]/net sales

Financial Ratios

Interest Cover	= operating profit/interest expense
Tangible Net Worth	= total net worth − intangibles
Working Capital	= total current assets − total current liabilities
Current Ratio	= total current assets/total current liabilities
Liquid Assets	= cash + short term investments + trade debtor + other debtors
Quick Ratio	= (liquid assets + prepayments)/total current liabilities
Gearing	= (total loans + std + cpltd)/total net worth
Leverage	= total liabilities/total net worth
Interest Cost	= interest expense/(total loans + std + cpltd)

Cash flow Ratios

Cash flow Interest Cover	= operating profit/Interest expense
Financing Payments Cover	= operating profit/(Interest expense + cpltd + dividends)
Debt Service Ratio	= operating profit/(std + cpltd + interest expense)
Total Debt Payout	= total interest − bearing debt/operating profit
Long term Debt Payout	= total interest − bearing ltd/operating profit

std = short term debt; cpltd = current portion of long term debt;
ltd = long term debt.

The quick ratio is a more accurate guide to liquidity, and is as follows:

$$\frac{\text{Current assets less inventories}}{\text{Current liabilities}}$$

The quick ratio excludes inventories and concentrates on cash, marketable securities and receivables. It is a conservative ratio that is not vulnerable to asset shrinkage (the fact that inventory may fetch less than its accounting value in a bankruptcy) and thus provides a more reliable (albeit weaker) measure of liquidity than the current ratio. Reality probably lies somewhere in between the two.

Debt ratios

Debt ratios are used to measure the indebtedness of companies. Several debt ratios may be used. The debt-to-net worth ratio is computed by simply dividing the total debt of the firm (including current liabilities) by its net worth.

$$\frac{\text{Total debt}}{\text{Net worth}}$$

When intangible assets are significant, they frequently are deducted from net worth to obtain the tangible net worth of the firm, since the valuation of intangibles is often a subjective exercise.

Coverage ratios

Coverage ratios measure the ability of a company to generate cash flow in excess of its financing commitments. Credit rating agencies make extensive use of these ratios. One of the most traditional of the coverage ratios is the cash flow coverage ratio, which may be expressed as:

$$\frac{\text{Annual cash flow before interest and taxes}}{(\text{Interest} + \text{principal payments})}$$

Bankers typically like to see a cash flow coverage ratio at a minimum of 150%. This ratio can be further refined to take into account the tax implications on cash flow:

$$\frac{\text{Annual cash flow before interest and taxes}}{(\text{Interest } + \text{ principal payments } [1/(1 - \text{income tax rate})])}$$

This ratio adjusts for the fact that interest payments occur before taxes whilst principal payments occurs after tax by including $[1/(1 - \text{income tax rate})]$. In such cases, it is essential to know the tax rate in the jurisdiction in question. For example, if the tax rate is 34% and annual principal payments are €100 000, before-tax earnings of €151 515 would be needed to cover these payments.

Sensitivity analysis

In any project finance cash flow forecast, certain assumptions are made. It is therefore necessary for the banker to assess the effect of potential impacts on key variables of the model such as shortfalls in the project's production, changes in the product price, increases in operating costs, fluctuations in interest rates, etc. The purpose of this is to test the ability of the project's cash flows to weather the storms of volatility and unexpected developments and identify possible corrective avenues. This process is known as sensitivity analysis.

The spreadsheet in Figure 3.5 illustrates a basic sensitivity analysis model concerning the building of a housing development in a Middle Eastern country. In some instances the ability of the borrower to service debt may be particularly sensitive to changes in one particular variable. The lender needs to identify and be aware of which elements these are so that rapid corrective action can be undertaken in the event that these problems manifest themselves. This is why in most credit proposals 'standard' and 'downside' scenarios are prepared – the latter (e.g. Figure 3.6) effectively depicts what would happen to the borrower's ability to repay the loan should extremely pessimistic assumptions materialize.

The credit officers of the bank may request that the combined effects of these changes are shown in the form of one ratio which demonstrates

Increase in house rent 9.0%[a]   DSR 130%[b]   Int. rate 6%[d]   Equity 1500[e]
Increase in land rent 0.0%[b]   Y1 Full rent 2340[b]   Y1 electr. 144[b]

	2004	2005	2006	2007	2008	2009	2010	2011	2012	2013
Occupancy[c]	40%	95%	95%	95%	95%	95%	95%	95%	95%	95%
Full occupancy[a]	2340	2551	2780	3030	3303	3600	3924	4278	4663	5082
	2004	**2005**	**2006**	**2007**	**2008**	**2009**	**2010**	**2011**	**2012**	**2013**
Construction costs	−6657[b]	−952[b]								
Legal fees	−200[b]									
Ground rent	−500[b]	−500	−500	−500	−500	−500	−500	−500	−500	−500
Rental income[c]	936	2423	2641	2879	3138	3420	3728	4064	4429	4828
Net elec. receipts[c]	58	137	137	137	137	137	137	137	137	137
Net operating cash flow	**−6363**	**1108**	**2278**	**2516**	**2775**	**3057**	**3365**	**3701**	**4066**	**4465**
Equity capital	1500[e]									
Loan	6800	1000	200							
NCF before finance	**1937**	**2108**	**2478**	**2516**	**2775**	**3057**	**3365**	**3701**	**4066**	**4465**
Loan outstanding	6800	7800	7200	6200	5200	4000	2000	0	0	0
Loan interest[d]		408	468	432	372	312	240	120	0	0
Loan			800	1000	1000	1200	2000	2000	0	0
Total fin. outflows	**0**	**408**	**1268**	**1432**	**1372**	**1512**	**2240**	**2120**	**0**	**0**
Net cash flow	**1937**	**1700**	**1210**	**1084**	**1403**	**1545**	**1125**	**1581**	**4066**	**4465**
Carryforward net	**1937**	**3636**	**4846**	**5930**	**7333**	**8878**	**10003**	**11583**	**15650**	**20115**
DS ratio		272%	180%	176%	202%	202%	150%	175%	NA	NA
DS ratio required		140%	140%	140%	140%	140%	140%	140%	140%	140%

Figure 3.5   Housing development cash flow sensitivity analysis model base case. Input variables are shown in the top rows, letters a–e show links between values entered in the spreadsheet

Increase in house rent 6.0%[a] DSR 130%[b] Int. rate 8%[d] Equity 1000[e]
Increase in land rent 0.0%[b] Y1 Full rent 2340[b] Y1 electr. 144

	2004	2005	2006	2007	2008	2009	2010	2011	2012	2013
Occupancy[c]	10%	80%	85%	85%	90%	90%	90%	90%	90%	90%
Full occupancy[a]	2340	2480	2629	2787	2954	3131	3319	3518	3730	3953
Construction costs	-6657[b]									
Legal fees	-200[b]									
Ground rent	-500[b]	-500	-500	-500	-500	-500	-500	-500	-500	-500
Rental income[c]	234	1984	2235	2369	2659	2818	2987	3167	3357	3558
Net elec. receipts[c]	14	115	122	122	130	130	130	130	130	130
Net operating cash flow	**-7109**	**648**	**1857**	**1991**	**2288**	**2448**	**2617**	**2796**	**2986**	**3188**
Equity capital	1000[e]									
Loan	6800	1000	200							
NCF before finance	**691**	**1648**	**2057**	**1991**	**2288**	**2448**	**2617**	**2796**	**2986**	**3188**
Loan outstanding	6800	7800	7200	6200	5200	4000	2000	0	0	0
Loan interest[d]		544	624	576	496	416	320	160	0	0
Loan			800	1000	1000	1200	2000	2000	0	0
Total fin. outflows	**0**	**544**	**1424**	**1576**	**1496**	**1616**	**2320**	**2160**	**0**	**0**
Net cash flow	**691**	**1104**	**633**	**415**	**792**	**832**	**297**	**636**	**2986**	**3188**
Carryforward net	**691**	**1795**	**2428**	**2843**	**3636**	**4468**	**4765**	**5401**	**8387**	**11575**
DS ratio		**119%**	**130%**	**126%**	**153%**	**151%**	**113%**	**129%**	**NA**	**NA**
DS ratio required	140%	140%	140%	140%	140%	140%	140%	140%	140%	140%

Figure 3.6 Housing development cash flow sensitivity analysis model downside scenario. Input variables are shown in the top rows, letters a–e show links between values entered in the spreadsheet

the ability of the borrower to service debt. The debt cover ratio fulfils this function and is a concept which is explained in the following case study and next section.

Housing development cash flow sensitivity analysis

In the following case study, the base case projected cash flows concern a housing development project in the Middle East. The financial projections for the housing project are presented by the sponsor to the lead bank. You are asked to check whether the cash flow cover for interest payable and debt repayment each year is acceptable.

For the purposes of analysis, and to assist in re-structuring the finance package, the bank decides that a minimum figure of 1.40 should be set for the debt service ratio (DSR). Considering the riskiness of the project, this should be sufficient to maintain acceptable cover in the event of adverse variations in constructing costs and rental income.

Working within this constraint the lead bank comes up with the base case cash flow projection.

Your bank, however, wants to test the new package by adversely flexing some of the input variables – increases in house rent, occupancy rates, rental income, interest rates and an additional equity injection. You hence modify certain of the key variables in the 'downside scenario'.

Accordingly, the model with the input variable zones enables various elements to be tested: for example

- house rents increase more slowly at 6% instead of say 9%;
- occupancy rates are lowered to 80–85–90% instead of 95%;
- interest rates rise from 6% to 8%;
- equity injections are lowered from 1500 to 1000.

In the spreadsheets in Figures 3.5 and 3.6 letters a–e denote direct associations between variables, with the input variables in the top rows.

The resulting effect on the cash flow is shown in the housing development cash flow sensitivity analysis downside scenario. This scenario is regarded as extremely pessimistic since multiple variables are tested simultaneously. This is normal since one can assume the agent bank is trying to sell the loan with optimistic projections.

We can see that the debt service ratio in the downside scenario dips below the mandated 1.4 but is still well above 1.0, thereby offering a margin of error.

An intelligently designed spreadsheet with the input variables concentrated in the upper zone as a 'dashboard' colour coded to the relevant areas in the spreadsheet enables quick testing of the impact that various input variables may have on the project cash flows. These can moreover be summarized in graphical form, as seen in Figures 3.7–3.10.

It is useful to consider the impact of changes in the input variables on the bank and on shareholders. This can help focus the inquiry for added security measures via covenants or guarantees.

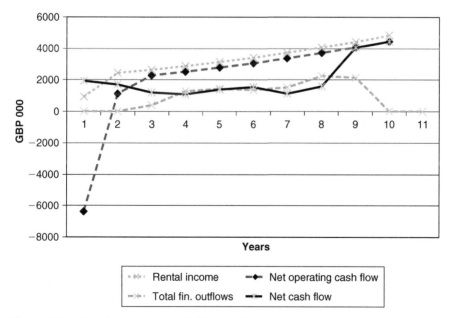

Figure 3.7   Housing project cash flow model: base case

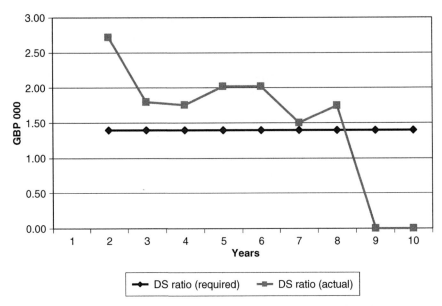

Figure 3.8 Housing project cash flow model: debt service ratio – base case

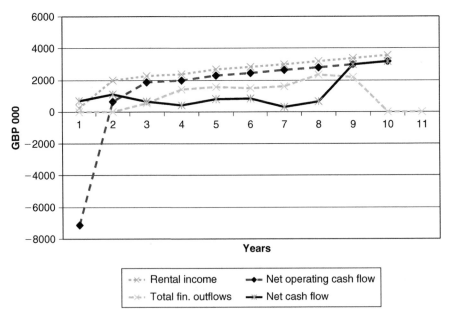

Figure 3.9 Housing project cash flow model: downside

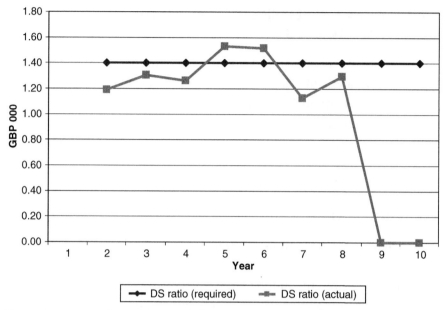

Figure 3.10   Housing project cash flow model: debt service ratio – downside

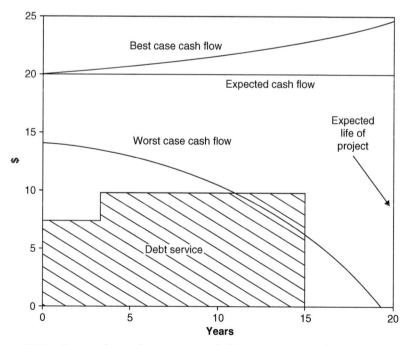

Figure 3.11   Comparison of expected cash flow, best case and worst case (constant dollars)

Credit risk appraisal: general considerations

Commercial lenders in a project financing supposedly conduct a detailed review and analysis of a proposed project before the decision to lend is made. While the intensity, scope and methodology of the credit analysis varies from institution to institution, there are general fundamentals that almost every bank applies to the credit decision. These are summarized below.

Pre-construction

- **Experience and reputation of project sponsor** The project sponsor's experience in similar projects is important to the lenders. Although each project presents unique risks, an industry reputation for project support and completion, 'on spec and on time', is evidence of a 'bankable' reputation.
- **Engineering and design** Lenders should assure themselves that any technology being used in the project is of a reliable and proven design, as evidenced by a solid track record of similar installations. Any potential weaknesses and successes in addressing those issues in other project financings should be noted. New technology, often for the sake of increased operating efficiency, should be carefully analysed for any potential weaknesses and this increased risk should be reflected in the facility pricing.
- **Construction** Even though a project's conceptual design may intend to limit the potential for construction difficulties, construction contracts that provide performance guarantees and warranties, as well as penalty and damage payments sufficient to ensure the project's acceptance within the established schedule and budget, are more acceptable to banks than projects that do not have such guarantees.

Post-construction

- **Operations and management** How an owner/operator plans to operate and maintain a facility during start-up and the early years of a project generally determines the long term performance of the facility.

Banks obviously prefer to see a management team with experience and a proven track record in management of the facility.

- **Experience and resources of operator**   The entity operating the project, typically pursuant to a long term operating agreement, must possess sufficient experience and reputation to operate it at the levels necessary to generate cash flow at projected levels. It also needs to have the necessary financial solidity to support operating guarantees and other contractual obligations.

- **Price and supply of raw materials**   The project must be assured of a supply of raw materials at a cost within the acceptable ranges of financial projections. This will depend on the availability of materials in the project area or need to source them from afar. Anything which can adversely impact this supply needs to be identified as a risk, and mitigated if possible.

- **Off-take contracts**   Since off-take contracts are the main source of project revenue, the lender will be particularly interested in the contractual documentation governing such agreements. The lender will be particularly interested in the payments under the contract being adequate to pay operating costs, and service the debt.

- **Equity contributions**   In many project financings, it is important to specify the contractual arrangements for the timing and certainty of the equity funding in order to optimally schedule the timing and dependability of the injection of funds into the project.

- **Value of project assets as collateral**   The project lender should ensure that the contracts enable assets to be assignable, since if there is a foreclosure, the contracts will only have value if they can be taken over by the lender and then sold (assigned) to a future buyer.

- **Competitive market exposure**   Given that most projects produce a generic commodity, low-cost production relative to the market is essential for an investment-grade rating. Indeed, experience has shown that off-take contracts providing stable revenues may not be enough to mitigate adverse market situations. Hence, market risk can potentially take on greater importance than the legal profile of, and security underlying, a project. The analysis of a project's competitive market position should therefore focus on factors such as industry fundamentals, commodity price risk, market outlook for demand and price, foreign exchange exposure and vulnerability to foreign devaluations, and the ease or difficulty with which new competitors may enter the industry.

■ **Counterparty exposure** Much of the project's strength derives from contractual participation of outside parties in the establishment and operation of the project structure. This participation raises questions about the strength or reliability of such participants. Traditionally, a project's credit strength is often linked to the credit strength of the off-take counterparty; this was especially the case for IPPs with power purchase agreements signed with a creditworthy entity, such as a utility. Important off-take counterparties to project now can include providers of LOCs and surety bonds, parties to interest rate and currency swaps, buyers and sellers of hedging agreements and other derivative products, marketing agents, political risk guarantors and government entities. Because projects have increasingly taken on complex structures, the failure of a counterparty can put a project's viability at risk. Accordingly, the analysis of counterparty risk not only becomes critical to a project's rating, it becomes more complicated. Whereas projects traditionally sold output to one buyer, projects may find that they have multiple buyers.

Financial strength

Overall project financial risks of course are larger than the risks measured by debt service coverage ratios. As we have seen, projects are subject to several varieties of financial threats over and above the ability of the project to generate stable and sufficient levels of cash flows. Negative impacts can arise from elements such as foreign exchange risks, inflation risks, liquidity risks and funding risks.

■ **Financial risk** Financial risks can in part be addressed by hedging against foreign exchange and interest rate movements via interest rate swaps, interest rate caps, collars and floors, etc. Debt servicing can be impacted by factors such as market prices, inflation rates, energy costs, tax rates, etc., all of which impact the cash flow available for debt servicing commitments even if off-take agreements are in place. Certain of these risks can be protected via hedging facilities such as forward sales and futures and options contracts, but this will also increase the overall cost of funding.

- **Capitalization and financial flexibility** Project sponsors will generally try to structure highly leveraged transactions in order to limit their equity commitment. Fundamentally, the amount of leverage is irrelevant to the credit rating, since repayment is conditional upon the project's ability to generate cash sufficient to cover financing commitments. Low leverage however is often considered an indication of creditworthiness, and is therefore essential for raising investment-grade rated debt. Amortization schedules also often influences the rating – the sooner the money is paid, the less the financial commitments stretch out over time, thus reducing risk and improving the credit risk rating of the facility.
- **Inflation risk** Inflation, or the lack of inflation, can pose several risks; for example, projects whose contractual revenues are linked to inflation risk being weakened if inflation falls below inflation assumptions. Basically, in such cases, revenues will fail to grow by the anticipated (inflation) rate and generate lower than expected cash flows. Inflation can also pose a threat if the raw materials and inputs of the project are subject to price hikes. It is important to identify and analyse these vulnerabilities in order to mitigate the risks.
- **Interest rate risk** Most project financings generally remove interest rate risk by financing with fixed interest rate debt. However, this is not always the case and some project financings rely on a floating reference rate. Such projects risk an erosion of their credit strength if market reference rates increase and revenues cannot increase at the same rate to offset the increased costs. It is therefore important to factor in such elements in sensitivity analyses in order to establish the margin of flexibility.
- **Liquidity risk** Liquidity is essential in order to maintain operations. Creditworthy projects should demonstrate the ability to generate sufficient cash to fund ongoing activities and debt servicing. Some projects however may need to have a working capital facility in order to even out revenues subject to seasonal variations.

Chapter 4

Contractual framework

General

The complexities of project finance are such that the project parameters and interrelations need to be managed within a clear framework, which is formalized via contracts. Project finance can therefore be subject to numerous subcontracts within the overall framework of the project financing. We consider below some of these contracts.

Pre-development agreements

Prior to commencing a project, several elements need to be already in place before the project can begin. Elements such as:

- **Licences and concessions** In many cases, implementing a project financing in its building as well as operating phases depends on obtaining the appropriate licences, permits and concessions from the government of the country in which the project is based. The government may negotiate certain clauses which give it the right to revoke the licence or concession. Lenders should therefore seek security via a variety of issues such as government approval of the financing and of the project, and enabling the lenders to take enforceable security, manage the project if necessary, and repatriate profits.
- **Concession agreements** Concession agreements create the right and obligation to build, own and eventually transfer back to the grantor infrastructure used for the general benefit of the population. Concession agreements should therefore clearly state the rights such as terms and duration of the concession, ability to extend the concession

even if there are changes in the law, termination of the concession should not be expropriatory, and banks should be able to freely transfer the concession to a third party.

■ **Shareholder agreements**   Given that interests differ, it is desirable to have a shareholder agreement in order to govern the relationship of the stockholders with respect to the project. Such agreements include management and voting; development, construction, and operating stage financing, working capital financing; amounts and dates of additional capitalization.

■ **Partnership agreements**   Where a general or limited partnership form of ownership of a project is selected by the project participants, this will be governed by a partnership agreement. The agreement will prohibit anything that has a substantial adverse impact on the project, such as taking on additional debt, amending or modifying the loan agreement or important project contracts; waiving rights to security, selling the project, etc. without the approval of a specified number of the partners.

■ **Joint venture agreements**   A JV agreement will govern the interrelations amongst the participants and specify issues such as the name and purpose of the JV, management and voting rights and other mechanistic aspects of the project to be defined, such as date and time of capital injections, transferability, sale, competition, etc.

Construction agreements

The banks' wish list for a construction contract is fairly standard and predictable, but it should include the following aspects:

■ The construction contract must be turnkey. No aspect of the construction and design should 'fall between the cracks'. So, there must be no nominated subcontractors or equipment specified by the project company (or, if there are, the contractor must take responsibility for the same).

■ There should be a fixed price, incapable of being reopened, and the price should be paid in one lump sum on completion.

■ Completion must occur within a fixed period.

■ The force majeure events should be limited.

- Liquidated damages should be payable if completion is not achieved by a fixed date and those liquidated damages should be adequate and at least cover interest payable on the loan.
- There should be no (or large) limits on the contractor's liability.
- The contractor should give extensive guarantees and, if the contractor is to be released from liability for defects after a period, that period should be long and only run from the passing of a well-defined completion test.

Contractors bonds

Contractors bonds provide ways of incentivizing or securing the performance of contractors, subcontractors and suppliers. The types of bonds are:

- **Bid (or tender) bonds**   These bonds require the bidder to pay a penalty should they be awarded the contract and decide to withdraw. This mechanism is designed to prevent fraudulent bids designed solely to deprive competitors the work.
- **Performance bonds**   These effectively guarantee performance by the contractor for a certain proportion (perhaps 5% or 10%) of the contract price.
- **Advance payment guarantees**   The project company may have to advance funds to enable the contractors to purchase materials and begin working on the contract. In such cases, the contractor will provide an advance payment guarantee which means that if they do not begin (or complete beginning) working on the project, that they will have to refund the advance granted.
- **Retention guarantees**   The construction contract might provide for the project company to retain a specified percentage of the progress payments, in order to repair defects which may not immediately be apparent. Conversely, the contractor wishing to receive full payment may instead offer a guarantee for the equivalent amount of the retention guarantee.
- **Maintenance bonds**   These are bonds to cover defects which are discovered after completion of construction. Upon materialization of the defect, the bonds will be used to rectify the defects. Similar cover can

also be obtained by extending the time frame of performance or retention bonds.

Operating and maintenance agreements

Sponsors try to mitigate supply risk via several mechanisms. The major provisions that lenders look for in operating and maintenance agreements are similar to those that the project company are concerned with. These include:

- **Supply-or-pay agreements**   Also known as 'put-or-pay', these arrangements require the supplier to either provide the requisite input or provide cash compensation to enable the project company to obtain the requisite input.
- **Sales/off-take agreements**   Projects generally try to minimize the effects of market volatility via off-take agreements. Such contracts should protect lenders from risk between the contracted price for the output and the market price. Mechanisms which can limit market risk include guaranteed capacity payments (sufficient to cover fixed and debt service costs) and guaranteed production levels.
- **Take-or-pay and take-and-pay contracts**   Take-or-pay and take-and-pay contracts can be defined as long term contracts to pay for goods over a long term at a fixed price whether or not delivery occurs. The idea is that the purchaser ensures a steady source of supplies at a fixed price and the seller obtains some relief from price and volume volatility. Typically, the amount of the payments under a take-or-pay contract should be sufficient to cover all – or a defined part – of the operating costs and financing payments. It is essential that the 'hell or high water' obligation upon the purchaser be ironclad and enforceable. The rights under this contract will usually be assigned to the lenders who will have a direct claim under it should the borrower experience payment shortfalls.
- **Throughput agreements**   The concept of a throughput agreement is very similar to a take-or-pay contract except it typically is used by a facility where goods transit such as a road, port, pipeline, rail track, etc. A typical example of a throughput project is the Baku Tbilisi Ceyhan pipeline project to transport oil from Azerbaijan to the Turkish

port of Ceyhan. In such a project, the parties enter a throughput agreement with the pipeline companies under which they agreed to pass sufficient oil and gas through the pipelines at agreed tariffs so that the cash earned would be sufficient to enable the pipeline companies to meet all of their financial obligations. Such arrangements can also be subject to a 'hell or high water' clause so that should it become impossible to pass oil or gas through a pipeline then cash payments would be made, equivalent to the amounts needed to enable the pipeline companies to meet their commitments.

Sponsor support agreements

In some cases, it becomes desirable to conclude sponsor support agreements. Some methods of providing sponsor support are:

- **Working capital, maintenance and cash deficiency agreements** These provide comfort similar to a completion guarantee, except that they can remain in place (maintenance) beyond the completion date.
- **Letters of comfort** Lenders typically require letters of 'comfort', 'support' or 'understanding' from the ultimate shareholders of the project company or other interested parties. The legal position of these 'letters of comfort' is often misleading since, in reality, no guarantee exists. These letters are basically exercises in window dressing since they are unenforceable in court. If the lenders are looking for more than 'moral commitment', this should be clearly stated and reflected in a clearly worded document vetted by lawyers. Conversely, if sponsors do not intend to provide a legal undertaking, this should also be clearly stated. Ambiguous 'letters of comfort' are not only misleading, they are indeed a waste of time.

Management agreements

In some projects, the management of the project entity is governed by a separate document in which a project manager is appointed to manage the project. The project management agreement typically imposes on the project company certain management conditions to be decided via negotiation. Typically, this might include management, preparing budgets and forecasts, financial and technical record keeping, reporting, construction management, etc.

Representations and warranties

The representation and warranty section of project contracts, including the project loan agreement, serves an important role in the project due diligence process. It basically confirms, legally, that certain conditions enabling the project to commence, are in place.

- A representation is a statement by a contracting party to another contracting party about a particular fact that is correct on the date when made. A representation is made about either a past or present fact, never a future fact. Facts required to be true in the future are covenants.
- A warranty is sometimes confused with a representation, but in practice the two terms are used together, the contracting party being asked to represent and 'warrant' certain facts.

Generally, a breach of a warranty could be enforced as a breach of contract. Because some courts blur the distinction between representations and warranties, the lenders typically require the borrower to 'represent and warrant' the same facts, and to state that the untruth of any representation or warranty *is* an event of default under the contract. It is important to note that linking this to an event of default enables the banks to exercise leverage over the borrower without necessarily having to initiate litigation.

The two main conditions underlying the initial representations and warranties are:

- to ensure that the legal status of the company exists, as this governs the ability to enforce the contract against a presumed set of assets, and
- to ensure that the contracting party is duly authorized to enter into the transaction (*ultra vires* – subject to any corporate or partnership restriction relating to the transaction).

Some lenders decide to verify this information as an added measure of prudence.

Project loan/credit agreements

Loan agreements define and regulate the financing instruments and interrelations amongst the various parties participating in the project financing. Loan agreements may be supplemented with an intercreditor agreement which defines the rights that the project creditors will have in a default, including step-in and foreclosure.

Another role of loan documentation is to ensure that the initial credit risk profile remains unchanged over the life of the facility. This is achieved by implementing various conditions and covenants in the loan agreement which define what the management can and cannot do.

Loan agreements, via financial or ratio covenants, can also be used to oblige the borrower to maintain certain parameters such as liquidity, cash flow and other elements which may adversely impact the borrower's (and project's) risk profile.

The typical project finance loan agreement will govern several elements:

■ mechanistic provisions (e.g. loan payments and repayments);
■ interest rates and provisions;
■ lender protection against increased costs and illegality;
■ representations and warranties;
■ events of default;
■ miscellaneous provisions, including submission to jurisdiction.

The credit agreement moreover will address matters that reflect the transnational nature of the transactions, e.g. waiver of sovereign immunity (in the case of projects with a government component); identification of the currency for debt repayments.

The goal of the project finance lender is to address the control over as many project risks as is possible. To the extent risks (economic/political) cannot be adequately regulated, these must be addressed in the interest rate and fee pricing of the credit.

Credit agreements – basic terms

Typically, terms of the credit agreement will include the following:

- **Conditions precedent** These would include the delivery of certified copies of the borrower's constitutional documents, of any relevant board and shareholder resolutions and of any key documents and the delivery of legal opinions confirming, *inter alia*, that the loan agreement was within the borrower's powers and had been properly authorized.
- **Conditions precedent to each drawdown** Specific conditions to satisfy prior to each drawdown of funds (e.g. obtaining a completion certificate or engineering progress report).
- **Drawdown mechanics** The specificities relating to drawdowns (approvals, account numbers, dates, prorate allocations, etc.).
- **An interest clause** Interest is charged by reference to base rate; the loan agreement should stipulate which bank's base rate is being used.
- **A repayment clause** A term loan may be repayable in one bullet repayment or in instalments of fixed or variable amounts.
- **Margin protection clauses** If a bank suffers an unexpected cost connected with making a loan, this will obviously erode its margin: Three main types of margin protection clause are included in loan agreements as a result: the gross-up clause, the increased costs clause and the market disruption clause.
- **The illegality clause** This clause states that, if it becomes illegal for a bank to continue to make loans or otherwise participate in the loan agreement, the borrower must prepay the loans made by that bank and the bank's obligations will be terminated.
- **Representations and warranties** If things go wrong, the banks simply want their money back and the best way to do this is to give them a debt (and not a damages) claim. This is done by making the breach of representation and warranty under the loan agreement an event of default (see below). The representations and warranties are often made 'evergreen', which means automatically renewable on a permanent basis.

- **Undertakings** These are things that the lender must do. A loan agreement will contain various undertakings from the borrower, ranging from the purely informative (e.g. provide annual accounts) to the financially protective (e.g. an undertaking not to create security in favour of third parties). The three key undertakings in a typical loan documentation are the **negative pledge**, an **undertaking not to dispose of assets** (unless waived) and an undertaking by the borrower **not to change its business**. The purpose of these undertakings is to force the borrower to keep the risk profile he had upon entering the transaction.
- **Events of default** Events of default in a typical loan agreement may include non payment, breach of representation and warranty, breach of covenant, insolvency and 'cross-default'. These are financial events of default which means that the borrower has failed to maintain or respect certain financial conditions. The cross-default clause basically comes into effect when the borrower defaults on borrowings or financial obligations with a third party. Since a cross-default is often an indication of serious financial problems, the cross-default clause enables the bank which is exposed to move to foreclose on the loan even if no default has occurred.

Significant provisions of the project finance credit agreement

The main provisions of project finance credit agreements are:

- **Additional indebtedness** Project-financed transactions, on occasion, need to issue additional debt for various purposes, such as capital improvements, cost overruns, changes in environmental or economic legislation, etc. It is important that the banks exercise control and therefore additional indebtedness should only be permitted if the banks grant their approval. Limitations on additional indebtedness therefore typically figure in a project finance loan documentation.
- **Distribution of dividends** In order to prevent funds from being siphoned out of the company, the loan documentation will typically put a limit on dividend payments. These limits will be defined in function of the borrower's financial ratios such as available cash flow to financing payments. Here, the stronger the cash flow coverage, the higher the limit of dividends permitted. It is important however to

have an overall cap on dividends in order to ensure that project proceeds are ploughed back into the company and not siphoned off steadily, resulting in long term weakening of the borrower.

- **Grace periods prior to default** Due to the complex multinational nature of project finance, it is possible that payment delays may arise due to the trustee having administrative difficulties. Therefore project lending documentation will also include grace periods for missed principal and interest periods. However, too much leeway may invite difficulties, this is why such grace periods should be no more than three to five days.

- **Restrictions on intercompany loans** Project finance is, by definition, based on the use of a non-recourse vehicle providing certain off balance sheet benefits to sponsors. In order to ensure that the financial balance of such an arrangement is not upset, banks will require that there be restrictions on intercompany loans. This is to prevent the project sponsors of manipulating and weakening the project entity by making transfers to and from reserve accounts etc.

- **Reserve accounts** Project financing documents typically require projects to maintain several accounts with the project trustee. This may include a reserve account, a debt service reserve account, or an environmental legislation reserve account. Complying with such reserve accounts ensures that the project entity is protected in the event of any future legislative or regulatory changes.

- **Insurance** Project financings should ensure that all operating company and machinery is covered by reputable (investment-grade rated) insurance companies. It would be an added plus if the insurance company's claims settlement procedures not extend indefinitely in an effort to improve its 'liquidity management'.

Covenants

Covenants are undertakings given by a borrower as part of a term loan agreement. Their purpose is to help the lender ensure that the risk attached to the loan does not unexpectedly deteriorate prior to maturity. Covenants may, for example, place restrictions on merger activity or on gearing levels. Breach of a covenant normally constitutes an event of default and, as a result, the loan may become repayable upon demand.

From the borrower's point of view covenants often appear to be an obstacle at the time of negotiating a loan and a burdensome restriction during its term. As mentioned, they may also precipitate default. In order to negotiate an appropriate set of covenants, however, it is important for the borrower to have an understanding of the logic underlying the lender's position.

In the first instance the lender is using covenants to protect itself against possible actions the borrower could take, especially in times of financial distress, which would damage the lender's position. These actions are looked at in more detail below. Taking this a stage further, however, it can be expected that if the lender is unable to achieve adequate protection via covenants it will seek compensation, for example by requiring a higher margin. In some instances the covenants ideally wanted by the lender may be unduly restrictive and it may therefore be cost-effective for the borrower to be prepared to pay more for a greater degree of freedom. In other cases, however, it will be possible to negotiate an economically acceptable set of covenants in return for more favourable terms elsewhere in the contract. In instances such as these, debt covenants can be of benefit to both lender and borrower.

The games borrowers play

What specific actions by borrowers are lenders seeking to protect themselves against? These can be classified as financing, dividend or investment decisions that it is feared borrowers may take to enhance their own financial position at the expense of that of the lenders.

- **Financing decisions** The borrower could dilute the claim of the lender in question by subsequently raising additional debt having an equal or even a prior claim over the company's assets. If the original lender did not allow for this eventuality, then the borrower will have gained at the expense of the lender's position having become more risky.
- **Dividend decisions** A loan may be extended in the expectation that the borrower will maintain existing dividend and reinvestment policies. However, the borrower may start to pay out dividends in excess

of those envisaged by the lender at the expense of capital spending, so reducing the lender's asset backing.

- **Investment decisions** Two contrasting problems are anticipated under this heading; a failure to undertake certain potentially profitable investments and an over-eagerness to embark on excessively risky ones.

- **Under investment** Take the example of a company in financial distress, i.e. one whose outstanding loans exceed its asset value. The shareholders of such a company may be unwilling to finance a profitable project if they perceive that most of the benefit will simply accrue to the creditors by way of reducing the shortfall in asset value. In effect this is the dividend payment problem under another guise. Excessive dividends entail an unexpected cash outflow whereas here shareholders are failing to inject funds into the business.

- **Increasing business risk** Continuing with the example of a financially distressed company, it could be advantageous to the shareholders to switch into investments or business projects that are riskier than those that were held at the time the original loan was made. This is because in the likely event that such a project will fail, given its high risk, the loss will be borne in the main by the company's creditors in the form of an even lower payout than they were going to receive in the first place. In the improbable event of a substantial profit, however, the bulk of the benefit will accrue to the shareholders because the creditors' claims cannot exceed a fixed amount. Given the originally shaky position of the company, an increase in business risk will thus benefit the shareholders and disadvantage the creditors.

In summary then, lenders negotiating term loans will be concerned that, once the facility is in place, borrowers may unexpectedly raise additional debt finance with an equal or prior claim; pay out excessive dividends; fail to adequately maintain asset levels; or increase the risk profile of the company's assets. These would all be ways of benefiting the borrower at the expense of the lender. Moreover they are particularly relevant in the context of financially troubled companies. This is for two reasons. First, the raising of excessive amounts of additional debt can itself hasten financial distress. Secondly, the dividend and investment policies described are most likely to benefit shareholders at the expense of lenders when the company is already in or approaching financial difficulties.

Functions of loan covenants

In the light of the above, it would appear that loan covenants have four key functions:

- To place some restraint on the danger that a company may become financially distressed. This is achieved, for example, by gearing limits.
- To provide the banker with an early warning if, nevertheless, a company is beginning to have problems or is significantly changing the nature of its operations.
- To limit the extent to which borrowers can take actions such as those described above, which they may be particularly tempted to do when approaching financial distress.
- Finally, if necessary, to trigger loan default.

Proponents of the use of covenants, emphasizing the early warning function of covenants, take the case further by arguing that well-designed covenants provide not only timely performance indicators but also open up lines of communication between borrower and lender. Thus covenants serve to advise the borrower of what elements are of particular concern to the bank in difficult times, and when the company may need the forbearance and possibly active support of its banks, covenants ensure that the banks are well informed, supportive and less likely to impose draconian measures on management which may serve to unnecessarily accelerate panic in the markets.

Drawbacks to loan covenants

It is, nevertheless, recognized that covenants are not a universal panacea for resolving lender–borrower conflicts. For example, at some time during the term of a loan a once-relevant covenant may require amendment due to a change in circumstances. However, this may be costly to achieve, especially where a company has many bilateral agreements all requiring amendment or a syndicated facility requiring a large majority, or even unanimity, to agree amendments. Also, contractual restrictions on management activity can turn out to be more costly than the damage they are intended to limit. This is partly because covenants are sometimes a very blunt tool for controlling certain management activities, in particular investment decisions. Furthermore, setting appropriate levels for ratio covenants is not a science. If the ratios are too loose they will fail to control for the matters discussed above. If they are too tight, they will place unnecessary restrictions on the borrower and may trigger an unwarranted default.

Guidelines for efficient covenanting

It is this recognition of both the costs and benefits of covenants that has led one writer to suggest three guidelines for efficient covenanting:

- Covenants place limitations on borrower action. Therefore, in return, they must be seen to provide lenders with an appropriate form of economic protection. For example, to what extent does the widely used borrowings/capital and reserves ratio, based as it is on balance sheet values, actually provide the lender with either a measure of asset backing or a reliable indicator of impending financial distress?
- Covenants should not be so extensive that the protection afforded to the lender is outweighed by the costs they impose on the borrower in terms of restrictions on management action. For example, it would be very difficult to design a covenant that would directly protect the lender from the under-investment problem described above. This is because it would be impossibly intrusive to monitor a company's failure to undertake particular investments. Instead it usually suffices to track investment policy indirectly, for example via minimum net worth or current ratio covenants.
- For any desired degree of lender protection the least restrictive covenant should be used.

The above points focus on the costs and benefits of covenanting. While it may not be possible to quantify these costs and benefits, it is suggested that they are useful guidelines to bear in mind when negotiating a contract.

Types of covenants

The main covenants usually found in UK bank loan agreements cover non-financial and financial covenants as well as events of default, which can be triggered by covenant violations.

- **Non-financial covenants** Four important non-financial covenants are:
  - Negative pledge: this prevents the borrower from giving some future lender prior security over its assets.
  - Guarantees provided by members of a group of companies for the debt of other members of that group.
  - An undertaking to supply the lender with periodical financial information. Over and above the annual audited accounts, management accounts are the most frequently required, often on a quarterly basis.
  - Restrictions on capital spending, acquisitions and asset disposals.
- **Financial covenants** The most common financial covenants used in UK bank lending stipulate minimum net worth, interest cover and gearing (ratio of borrowings to net worth). Current ratio, cash flow ratio (e.g. cash flow interest cover) and asset disposal/net worth covenants are also used, although less frequently. By way of contrast, gearing and asset disposal/asset covenants tend to predominate in UK bond and debenture issues, whereas direct dividend restrictions are common in US private lending agreements.

Events of default

Events of default are those events, which, should they occur, permit the lender to require all amounts outstanding to become immediately payable. The typical events of default clauses are:

- Failure to pay amounts owing to the lender when due.
- Failure by the borrower to perform other obligations under the loan agreement. It is due to this clause that a covenant violation triggers an event of default.
- Any representation or warranty made by the borrower proving to be untrue.
- Cross-default, i.e. where the borrower has triggered an event of default or has actually been put into default on any other loan agreement.

■ Where a 'material adverse change' has occurred in the borrower's financial or operating position. This is clearly a catch-all clause and there is a view that where a company has negotiated a meaningful set of covenants, it can legitimately refuse to accept a continuing material adverse change clause.

Project financing covenants

Because of the complexity of project finance, covenants in a project finance transaction are more complicated than those of a standard syndicated loan. They must cover all possible eventualities. The covenants are designed to:

■ Ensure that the project company constructs and operates the project in the manner contemplated in the technical and economic assumptions that are the foundation of financial projections.
■ Provide the lender with advance or prompt warning of a potential problem, whether political, financial, contractual or technical.
■ Protect the lender's liens. These include covenants that the project will be constructed on schedule, within the construction budget and at agreed-upon performance levels; be operated in accordance with agreed standards; that project contracts will not be terminated or amended; and comply with operating budgets approved by the lender.

Covenants in a project finance loan agreement include many of the same covenants required by lenders in asset based loan transactions. However, unlike asset based transactions, project finance loan documents are designed to closely monitor and regulate the activities of the project company. Hence, there may be a bespoke nature to the covenants, the variety of which are only limited by the characteristics of the project being financed. Some of these are summarized below:

■ **Reports on project construction and completion** Progress reports are important in confirming that the project is proceeding as planned. These reports typically contain information on construction progress generally; status of equipment orders, deliveries and installation;

construction progress meetings; force majeure events; and target completion dates. Completion categories include *mechanical completion* (when the project is completed to the project specifications), *operation completion* (when the project is operated at the levels guaranteed in the construction contract, and within environmental requirements), and *final completion* (when all provisions of the construction contract have been performed and the last minor portions of the work such as clean-up completed).

- **Notice of certain events** Project finance loan agreements may contain provisions obligating the borrower to provide notice of certain events, including litigation, defaults, termination, cancellation, amendment, supplement or modification of any governmental permit, licence or concession, in order to provide the banks with advance notice so that corrective measures can be adopted.
- **Maintain existence** This is to avoid the phenomenon of 'intentional bankruptcy' – the borrower will agree to take all action necessary to preserve its existence. This means making required filings with governmental authorities and observing corporate or partnership formalities according to the laws of project company's home country.
- **Maintain interest in project** The project company will be obligated to maintain its ownership of the project for a negotiated period. This provides the lender with some comfort that the original equity investors will continue to be involved in the project.
- **Pay taxes** All taxes and other governmental charges must be paid when due and payable.
- **Compliance with laws** The project company will agree to comply with all laws applicable to it and to the project.
- **Obtain and maintain all approvals, permits and licences** The project company will obtain and maintain all approvals, permits and licences necessary or advisable in connection with the project.
- **No merger or consolidation** The project company will agree not to merge with or consolidate with any other entity. This is to ensure that the money is actually lent to the project entity and that the credit risks are not radically altered.
- **Engineering standards for construction and operation** The project company commit to maintaining a specified standard of care and operation, typically 'in accordance with good industry practice'.

- **Maintenance of properties**   The borrower typically commits to maintain the projects and the assets in good working order.
- **Environmental compliance**   The project company typically agrees to comply with the laws of the jurisdiction in which the project is located.
- **Insurance and insurance proceeds**   The project company will be required to obtain and maintain insurance to satisfy the requirements of the lender concerning form, creditworthiness of insurers, and suitability of named insured, loss payee and subrogation provisions, and other concerns.
- **Adhere to project performance documents**   The project company should agree to perform its obligations, and comply with each of the project documents, and not to intentionally create an event of default.
- **Amendment, modification, termination, replacement, etc. of project documents**   The project company will agree not to amend, modify or terminate, replace or enter into any project contract without the consent of the project lender.
- **Change orders**   Generally, significant changes, however, must be reviewed by the lenders to determine whether they affect the construction costs, schedule and reliability of the project and, if so, ensure that they do not cause an event of default.
- **Change of business**   The project company will agree not to engage in any business other than that assessed in the initial analysis – this is to avoid modifying the risk profile of the transaction.
- **Indebtedness**   Additional debt is not permitted without the approval of the project lenders. This is to avoid having the company's debt service capability unduly eroded.
- **Investments**   The project company is prohibited to make any investments unless approval has been granted by the lenders.
- **Dividends and restricted payments**   Released profits to the sponsors should be closely controlled by the project lender. Once the money is released, the funds are not typically available for use at the project. Release of profits is typically conditioned, there not being any default and all amounts required to be on deposit in various reserve accounts being present and the debt service ratios being adhered to.
- **Mandatory prepayment on the occurrence of certain events from excess cash flow**   Project finance credit agreements typically contain

mandatory prepayment sections to allow the lender to have a priority claim on cash flow before any transfers can be made to the sponsors.

■ **Financial tests** Financial tests, such as debt service coverage ratios, minimum working capital requirements, net worth and the like, are the subject of negotiations that are typically tailored to the specific risks of the project. Financial tests can provide early indications of difficulties. One such test is the debt service coverage ratio; however, it is seldom viewed by project lenders as the only necessary covenant.

■ **Special milestone dates** These may include dates that relate to construction deadlines and termination dates under off-take purchase agreements. These are incorporated into the loan agreement with covenants requiring the borrower to take required actions if the action has not been completed by the date specified.

■ **Change in the project** The company may be prohibited from changing or altering the project. In such cases, the definition of 'changes' should be clearly defined in the loan documentation. Changes for example consist not only of the type of business but also the scale or production volumes.

■ **Project support** The borrowers may require that the project company supports the project in all respects, including completion.

■ **Financial reporting** This covenant requires the company to provide appropriate accounts to the lenders: audited annual statements, interim statements, pro forma statements, quarterly or monthly statements, internal management accounts, etc. It is essential to specify if the statements are to be audited, and if so, in accordance with internationally recognized standards (e.g. IAS).

■ **Use of proceeds** The project company will covenant that loan proceeds will be used only for their intended purpose (to be specified in the loan documentation). The project lender will want to avoid any use of proceeds for unapproved project changes or uses since that may be construed as assuming the liability in event of liquidation.

■ **Security documents** The borrower will covenant that it will take all action required to maintain and to preserve security structures created by the lenders.

■ **Operating budget** The project company is typically required to submit an annual project operating budget within 60 days of the beginning of the next financial year for approval by the lenders.

- **Trustee accounts**   It is typical for all project revenues to flow through a revenue control account maintained by a trustee. This enables the lenders to monitor the income flows into the project. The borrower should therefore be required to establish this account and have all payments made to it transit via these accounts as a condition precedent to the loan agreement.
- **Capital expenditures**   Similar to investments, the project company is prohibited from making capital expenditures for the project, unless approval is granted by the lenders. This is to avoid any siphoning or diverting of funds earmarked for the project.
- **Transactions with affiliates**   Because the lender places restrictions on when profits can be distributed to the project sponsors, indirect distributions (for example, transactions with affiliates) are similarly disallowed.
- **Construction cost overruns**   In the event of cost overruns, the loan documentation should oblige the project company to apply those funds in a specific order, often reserving for the last application the most expensive options for the project.
- **Other covenants**   The loan agreement may contain other covenants, such as compliance with pension laws; limits on lease agreements; limits on sale and leaseback transactions, property disposals and transfers, etc.

NPVs and cover ratios

Cover ratios have several applications in the credit agreement. There may be an event of default if a cover ratio in the loan agreement is breached. This may suspend or prevent the borrower from effecting subsequent drawdowns under the loan facility. Moreover, the interest margin payable by the borrower may vary depending in function of the cover ratio level.

There are several types of cover ratios and each can have a specific purpose in the project financing loan documentation:

- **The project life cover ratio**   This ratio measures the NPV of the project to bank debt outstanding on any particular day.
- **The loan life cover ratio**   This ratio measures the NPV of the projected revenues during the period it is estimated that the bank debt will

remain outstanding (the 'loan life NPV') to bank debt outstanding on any particular day.

■ **The drawdown cover ratio**　This ratio measures the loan life NPV to the total to be borrowed from the banks (the 'peak debt amount'). If this cover ratio is used, it will be precedent condition to the drawdown of any loan that the required drawdown cover ratio is not breached.

■ **The repayment cover ratio**　This ratio measures how much needs to be repaid under a credit agreement on any given repayment date. A borrower would be required to repay an amount to ensure that the repayment cover ratio would be within its required level (say 1.75:1). This ratio can also be used as a trigger to an event of default, e.g. if the ratio falls to say below 1.4:1.

Control accounts

Control accounts enable the bank to control withdrawals by the borrower. Such accounts typically gather all payments to the company and enable the banks to exercise control over payments from the account. Banks will have security over any control accounts maintained in connection with the credit agreements. Such control accounts are typically structured as in the trustee accounts in Figure 2.3 'Project financing supported by a throughput contract'. Some types of control accounts are:

■ **Disbursement account**　The proceeds of all loan drawdowns and of all equity subscriptions would be paid into a disbursement account. Withdrawals would be permitted to fund construction costs. Disbursement accounts are used when banks want to control the disbursement or advancement of funds to the borrower. Withdrawals typically are subject to producing agreed supporting documentation (receipts or orders).

■ **Proceeds account**　All project revenues should be paid into a proceeds account and withdrawals, whether for operating purposes or dividend payments, made contingent upon obtaining approval from the lenders. This is to ensure that funds are not siphoned off to the benefit of the sponsors and weaken the project entity.

■ **Compensation account**　Compensation accounts are designed to isolate compensation payments (e.g. equipment damage, insurance claims, etc.), again, so that the lenders can monitor the flows into the project and ensure that the funds do not end up in the wrong place.

- **Debt service reserve account**   Debt service accounts are designed to create a reserve fund which is used to make interest and principal repayments should the project cash flow exhibit unforeseen adverse variations (e.g. a production blockage).
- **Maintenance reserve account**   This account is designed to build up a reserve to cater to cyclical maintenance of the project (say five or six years in the case of power plants). Banks would seek to ensure that funds be set aside from ongoing operations in order to be able to service the infrastructure at given intervals.

Events of default

Events of default in a project financing are similar to those in any classic commercial lending situation. These include technical defaults (representation and warranties, notices, delivery of financial information, notice that a subsidiary has disposed of assets, creation of liens), financial events of default (violation of a financial ratio covenant) and mechanistic events of default (non payment of interest or principal). Many of the events of default in a project finance credit transaction are due to poor housekeeping, some are minor warning signals, and others indication of deep-seated problems. Events of default specific to project finance transactions and not typically present in commercial lending include:

- **Payment**   As in any loan agreement, non-payment of interest or principal constitutes an event of default. Since project finance is unlike most other types of financing, the creditworthiness of third parties can affect the financing. Accordingly, payment defaults by another project participant under a project financing may be included as a credit agreement default.
- **Breach of covenants**   A breach of one of the covenants is obviously an event of default. The lenders can then assess the defaults on a case by case basis, and decide whether they are remediable or whether they warrant intervention or, *in extremis*, restructuring.
- **Breach of representation or warranty**   A breach of a representation or warranty set forth in the credit agreement also constitutes an event

of default. It is up to the banks to determine whether such a breach poses a serious threat to the project's viability.

■ **Filing of bankruptcy petition**   If any of the parties in a project financing (the project company, sponsors, contractor, operator, off-take purchaser or supplier), files a petition for bankruptcy or takes similar action, it is an event of default. This enables the banks to adopt early corrective actions.

■ **Judgments**   Final judgments rendered against the project company, any project sponsor or any major project participant are considered an event of default should they be in excess of a negotiated minimum amount. Like other events of default that include entities other than the project company.

■ **Final acceptance date**   If the project completion date, typically called the final acceptance date, does not occur by a certain date (based on the construction schedule agreed to in the construction contract and on the milestone dates in major project contracts, such as an off-take purchase agreement.), this can be considered an event of default.

■ **Government approvals**   Failing to obtain, maintain, renew, or replace government approvals or permits can also be considered an event of default. The borrower will naturally seek to limit the coverage of any such events of default to events that threaten the viability of the project or ability to perform its obligations under the credit agreement.

■ **Abandonment**   Abandonment of the project by the project company is an event of default.

■ **Expropriation**   An expropriation, whether a complete taking or an act of 'creeping expropriation', is an event of default.

■ **Ownership and control**   Failure of the project sponsors to maintain either an agreed-upon ownership interest or voting control of the project company is an event of default. The purpose of this clause is to ensure that the original equity investors remain committed to the project, maintaining the original risk profile.

■ **Payment of obligations**   If the project company, any project sponsor or any major project participant, such as the contractor, operator, off-take purchaser or supplier, defaults in a payment obligation in excess of a specified amount, this can be considered an event of default. The borrower will want to limit the reach of this event of default to only those failures that could reasonably be expected to have a material adverse effect on the project, or the borrower's ability to perform its obligations under the credit agreement.

■ **Breach of credit support**   If any party to a credit support document, such as the sovereign under a sovereign guarantee, or any credit support obligation under a project contract, is not paid when due, this will constitute an event of default. Providers of subordinated debt and parties obligated to make capital contributions are included in the scope of this default.

■ **Security documents**   If any security document, such as a security agreement, stock pledge agreement or mortgage, ceases to be in full force, or is no longer effective to create a first priority lien on the collateral, then an event of default occurs.

Conditions precedent to closing

Before a lender agrees to advance funds to a project company it will require that the borrower satisfies certain conditions known as 'conditions precedent'. Typical conditions precedent are detailed below:

■ **Host government concessions and licences.**
■ **Off-take agreements.**
■ **Supply agreements.**
■ **Construction contract and issuance of the notice to proceed.**
■ **Operation and maintenance agreements.**

The above elements all need to be in a form acceptable to the lender, be authorized, executed and delivered to the project company by the operator, and be enforceable against the operator in accordance with its terms.

■ **Permits**   The lender will require certified copies of all governmental actions, filings, permits and approvals necessary for the ownership, construction, start-up and operation of the project and the related facilities.

■ **Insurance and insurance consultant's report**   The lender will require copies of all insurance policies required by the terms of the credit agreement and the other project documents.

■ **Real estate**   Where available, it is customary for the lender to obtain land surveys of, and title insurance on, the project site and other real estate interests important to the project.

- **Financial statements of project company, project sponsors, guarantors and major project participants**   These must be submitted to the lender in order to assist the lender in determining whether these entities are sufficiently creditworthy to perform their role in the project financing.
- **Construction budget and construction drawdown schedule**   Periodic reporting on these elements enables the borrower to monitor the project during the construction period, including costs required to complete the project and funds available to do so.
- **Construction reports**   A report prepared by an construction firm acceptable to the lender must be submitted. This report analyses technical and economic feasibility of the project.
- **Consultants' reports**   Specialist reports are often required by the banks in order to enable them to assess technical minutiae which they are unfamiliar with.
- **Environmental review**   In most countries, project lenders will require some form of environmental audit and report by an environmental consultant.
- **Legal opinions**   Lawyer's opinions are needed to ensure that due diligence has actually been performed by competent, careful counsel. Legal opinions address matters such as due organization, due authorization, ability to execution and delivery of financing and project documents, enforceability and conformance with legislation.
- **No material adverse change**   On the closing date, there must be no material adverse change in the financial condition of the project sponsors, or any related parties.
- **No defaults**   The borrower must certify that there does not exist, on the closing date, any default or event of default under any of the project contracts.
- **No litigation**   The borrower must certify that there is no litigation in existence which relates to the project or its various participants.

Intercreditor agreement

Intercreditor agreements are used where there is more than one class of debt and where those classes of debt have different interests in the same collateral. The intercreditor agreement also generally provides that only the agent bank is authorized to negotiate on behalf of the participating banks and grant waivers to the borrower. This is to prevent individual banks from initiating individual actions.

Security agreements

Lenders' security concerns

The main issue concerning lenders regarding security is the ability to take effective control over the contracts and keep them in place to enforce security. There are several documents do to this.

Security documents

Some of the documents that might need to be entered into to create or record the required security interest are:

■ mortgages or fixed charges over land, buildings and other fixed assets;
■ fixed and/or floating charges over moveable assets, and production/ work in progress;
■ assignments of rights under underlying project documents (e.g. construction contracts, performance bonds, licences and joint venture agreements);
■ assignments of project insurances and brokers' undertakings;
■ assignments of sales contracts, take-or-pay, throughput or tolling agreements escrow accounts to control cash flows relating to the project;
■ assignments of long term supply contracts;
■ assignments of project management, technical assistance and consultancy agreements;
■ pledge of shares of project company, including charge over dividend rights.

Security on specific tangible assets

In many projects there will be some specific tangible assets. It is unlikely that the realisable value of such items in a project financing would be of great significance in relation to the overall debt, but they do have value. The assets specifically charged will usually include the following:

- **The tangible assets used in the facilities,** e.g. oil production equipment, machinery and other moveable assets.
- **Fixed assets (land, buildings and other fixtures of the project).** Since foreign lenders may not be able to acquire interests in property, it may be necessary to develop a security structure with local financial institutions to hold the security for the benefit of the syndicate via sharing arrangements.
- **The licence or other operating permits.** These are usually required to be held by a local national and are therefore not usually assignable or transferable without the host government's approval.
- **Technology and process licences.** Lenders will want to be able to transfer the rights to technology or process licences in order to be able to sell the business as a going concern. It is important not to separate the two since the technology may be worthless without the business assets and vice versa.

Chapter 5

Project financing in the economy

Project financing and the privatization agenda

By the early 1980s, project finance became a clearly identifiable profitable subsector of the banking world's revenue streams. From airport projects and nuclear power projects in Iraq, copper extraction in Brazil, to extracting oil and gas in Cameroon, and basing petrochemical facilities in developing countries with nascent legal codes, banks were lending billions of dollars to finance the extraction of natural resources from developing countries.

Two key factors have fuelled the substantial increase in the use of project financing techniques over the past two decades.

- First, the developed economies' tremendous demand for cheap energy and mineral resources, and the meeting of such demand by exploiting natural resources in poor countries with weak governments, typically in diverse and remote geographical areas.
- Second, the massive transfer of capital, predominantly debt capital, to the poor countries (euphemistically known as emerging markets). An undoubted factor here is that these countries often have only nascent legal systems, which is an incentive to multinational corporations to abandon less profitable economic activities in home countries that are more greatly regulated.

Until the early 1970s, much of the financing of infrastructure development in emerging countries came from government sources, such as the host country government, multilateral institutions and export financing agencies. The shift towards using private sources of capital is the logical result of the ideological agenda underpinning privatization and the roll-back of the state on the presumption that it is an impediment to progress and the will of human beings as manifested in elections, and public policy is an impediment to economic efficiency. We recall US ideologue Grover Norquist's words on the role of the state, who says 'I don't want to abolish government. I simply want to reduce it to the size where I can drag it into the bathroom and drown it in the bathtub' (http://www.atr.org/atrnews/052501npr.html). This provides the backdrop to explain the privatization agenda, which depends on project finance techniques.

Economic models fostered by the IMF and credit rating agencies, both nominally appendages of the US politico-economic system, meant that there was an increasing pressure to rely on private sources of capital. Moreover, the issues of sovereign risk as perceived by the US credit rating agencies who control access to the international financial markets meant that states were reluctant to tap the financial markets for fear of having their credit ratings lowered and access to financial capital made difficult due to increased costs or lowered credit ratings. The granting of, or level of credit ratings, moreover, appears at times to be linked to the various peregrinations of US foreign policy goals.

Geoff Anderson, in 'Standard bearers for the markets: international credit rating agencies, new actors in politics and public policy in the Australian states' (PhD, Flinders University, in progress) argues that this has significant implications for the development of public policy and the management task within the public sector. It also gives rise to a further set of issues surrounding the relationship between governments and the rating agencies. In particular, how the threat of a downgrade or promise of an upgrade has been used by governments as part of their political communication strategy both externally to the electorate and internally to the public sector. And what of the agencies themselves, how valid is their approach and methodology?

Anderson notes that the use of comments by rating agencies to pursue a particular political agenda is discussed by Hayward and Salvaris (1994) in their article 'Rating the states: credit rating agencies and the Australian state governments' (*Journal of Australian Political Economy*, vol. 34, no. 16), which also raises some questions concerning the agencies' methodology. Andrew Fight's *The Ratings Game* (Chichester: John Wiley and Sons, 2001) has a more extended, and damning, critique of the way the agencies operate. The role of ratings in shaping the 'image' of a government is discussed by Michael Kunczik (2002) in 'News media, images of nations and the flow of international capital with special reference to the role of rating agencies', *Journal of International Communication*, 8, no. 1.

While the trade press attributes this trend to the belief that the private sector is 'more efficient than multilateral institutions and public entities in infrastructure development' (without defining what 'efficient' means or providing proof of same), the reality is that it has been a concerted 20 year campaign by business-politico partners in partnership with credit rating agencies to impose models leading to the dismantling of the state and state legislation block by block and by all means possible, whether media, regulatory, competition legislation or the financial yardsticks used by US appointed arbiters of the international financial markets, and apply pressures to espouse economic mechanisms developed in the USA and fostered by the US business-politico network. Very little of the arguments espousing the efficiency of the private sector are grounded in economic facts but they are presented as such in a media and financial press that exhibits the objectivity and investigative acumen of the '*Völkischer Beobachter*'.

With the penalization of the state in getting involved in infrastructure projects, especially poor states with weak and typically non-elected governments, it is hardly surprising that they try to avoid the accusations of state interference in the economy by conforming to the established status quo and relying on more expensive and demanding private capital.

Indeed, this heralds the weakening of national sovereignty and its subservience to the exigencies of transnational private capital, with its short term commercial focus rather than any electoral mandate. Juxtaposing such short termism (indeed, the banks are subject to this short termism via the rating and share analysts who issue various pronouncements on the share price and creditworthiness of these banks) upon infrastructure projects of a long term nature obviously leads to a skewed appreciation of what properly constitutes long term sustainable development.

It also leads to notable fiascos such as the California energy collapse fostered by Enron, the privatization of Britain's third world rail network, or deficit-ridden Eurotunnel. That, however, is another story. The key point is that the confluence of these events means that there has been a shift in financing from the state to the private sector.

It is fair to say that this shift is not the result of careful consideration or performance assessment but rather is ideological in nature, coercive in its implementation and rapacious in its distribution of lucrative fees to consultants, accountants, lawyers, bankers and credit rating agencies, who present themselves as the agents of economic efficiency.

In the meantime, if natality rates fall, morality rates increase, communities and transport systems collapse and incidents of deteriorating hygiene and epidemics manifest themselves, this does not figure in the corporate media like CNN, or Bloomberg as it is irrelevant, if not detrimental to the propagation of an upbeat soundbite. For the apparatchiks of newly constituted states, power and the maintenance of attendant privileges, all too often fuelled by bribes and the transfusion of foreign aid projects, are more important than addressing issues of public dissatisfaction, especially when no electoral mandate is necessary to maintain power. Parties objecting to the imposition of such agendas are given meaningless labels such as 'anti-democratic' or 'terrorist'.

Newly constituted states in Central Asia, operating in an imploded vacuum with no inherited state sector, are natural candidates for being dragooned to this new world order, presented to a disenfranchised populace as 'progress' from the previous 'inefficient' systems.

The strongman of oil-rich Azerbaijan, straddling the strategic Caspian to Mediterranean BTC (Baku Tbilisi Ceyhan) pipeline route, and the

US-groomed English-speaking president of Georgia (where the pipeline continues its meanderings to the Mediterranean) provide an interesting illustration of how to establish the appropriate conditions precedent for a project financing. In 2003, Mr Aliyev, son of the deceased octogenarian former president of Azerbaijan, squeaked past the post in a contested election which US observers deemed did not warrant a vote recount since Mr Aliyev Jr did not 'request' one. In neighbouring Georgia, by contrast, the 2003 election irregularities resulting in the re-election of another octogenarian, Eduard Shevardnadze, to the Presidency were rapidly spotted by US observers and new elections 'arranged under international election monitors' since this was an amenable pretext to legally oust the recalcitrant apparatchik in favour of the younger and anti-Russian US protégé Saaskavili.

At the time of going to press, we have again seen the application of the 'democracy franchization process' in Ukraine, where a media savvy opposition and marketing apparatus contested the legitimacy of the 2004 elections (coincidentally supporting the US agenda of bringing Central Asian oil to market bypassing Russia) funded by US aid money to the tune of US$ 65 million (Associated Press, 11 December 2004).

The developed world's incessant appetite for raw materials such as oil, combined with the emergence of China as a key energy consumer for example, offers the prospect of even more brutal competition and manipulation of governments for these resources. The Iraqi geopolitical projects of President George Bush against the backdrop of 'peak oil' set the tone for the future.

As the project finance market matures, so the number of refinancings of project loans increases. This can be due to several reasons. First is that the project financing occurs at the early stage of the project when the risk is higher. As projects come on stream and the risk profile decreases this may warrant negotiating a new refinancing facility in order to lower funding costs. Secondly, the financial restrictions may be less restrictive than the risk control measures incorporated in the initial project finance documentation. These restrictions may be in financial ratio terms as well as in the ability of the now operating project company to enter into new business arrangements. Finally, the banks may wish to modify their commitments based upon a reassessment of the risk and remuneration of the on-stream project.

Competition between banks for this lucrative business is increasing. Traditionally, private commercial banks have been the largest source of funds. New banks, however, are targeting this sector and developing new relationships in order to generate loan business. These newcomers (including quasi-sovereign banks) are naturally willing to accept greater risks than private commercial banks in an effort to break into the market. This competition has led to thinner lending margins, less stringent collateral requirements, more generous maturity schedules and possibly greater credit risk.

The private sector lenders naturally take a dim view of these gatecrashers, and claim that this unwelcome competition threatens the stability of the market. A more likely explanation is that they resent the newcomers upsetting a cartelized market with well-established pecking orders.

The project finance environment will be meeting new ambiguities and challenges. As the botched British Rail privatization and Enron meltdown illustrate, continuing to rely on the private sector to deliver on mission critical infrastructural requirements in order to satisfy ideological imperatives is rapidly becoming an expensive indulgence with, indeed, little value added, since no coherent long term development is possible. Extending the Private Finance Initiative (PFI) to every appendage of the state such as schools, hospitals and prisons will not only run out of steam in a limited market but rapidly generate its own obvious set of contradictions as it becomes evident the private sector is no better equipped to run reliable mission-critical services than the state, and indeed possibly worse. Mentioning the state of the British railways and rail maintenance for example rapidly brings to mind the word that no one dares utter – nationalization.

Pursuing ideological imperatives in the face of contradicting evidence can only be a short term phenomenon since the resultant logical contortions will become increasingly evident to all and foster its own set of contradictions.

Looking abroad, the current volatile environment of franchised democratic movements, crusades and jihads continues to cloud the political and country risk concerns of lenders and render risk assessment of new transactions difficult. Sustaining market demand for such high risk loans remains a speculative endeavour at best, while, with all eyes are now looking covetously to the Gulf and Iraq, the long term realities may impose their own order.

Project finance tables

The following tables illustrate the positioning of project financing as a component of overall bank lending.

Table 5.1 is interesting in that it conforms that the main industry sectors for borrowing are the financial sector (typically refinancing existing debts into more advantageous structures) and the 'big 4' of infrastructure categories (power, telecommunications, oil and gas, and transportation). The next major sectors are domestic consumer-driven retail trades and construction activity.

Tables 5.2–5.4 are all broadly similar with the observations made in Table 5.1, with the exception that Computers figure prominently in Asia Pacific, no doubt driven by the fact that this geographic zone is the major manufacturing centre for IT equipment. Despite the fact that much computer equipment features the logos of well-known Western companies, the reality is that the components are manufactured to specifications by Asian manufacturers, who require considerable investment in plant and infrastructure.

The UK PFI model

The Private Finance Initiative (PFI) was launched by the UK government in 1992 as another step in the dismantling of the state, seen as an impediment to economic efficiency and unfettered speculation since it

Table 5.1   Industry volume table for global syndicated loans in 2003

	Total amt (US$ m)	No.
Finance	283 892	596
Utility and power	178 139	361
Telecommunications	148 113	229
Oil and gas	121 299	348
Retail	93 053	269
Transportation	91 488	285
Real estate	88 030	418
Automobile	86 962	136
Construction/building	71 699	308
Food and beverage	69 765	214
Healthcare	68 950	242
Insurance	66 046	110
Computers	62 558	287
Consumer products	58 349	193
Services	51 027	206
Leisure and recreation	44 663	110
Metal and steel	43 346	148
Chemicals	42 130	161
Publishing	37 589	72
Dining and lodging	32 949	76
Forestry and paper	29 489	79
Holding companies	27 415	55
Government	19 813	54
Machinery	19 569	103
Mining	18 781	68
Aerospace/aircraft	16 668	20
Defence and aerospace	16 285	19
Other	13 340	29
Textile	10 521	84
Agribusiness	6 142	29
Unclassified	561	5
Total	1 918 631	5 311

Source: Dealogic, 2003

is not sufficiently under the control of private capital. By 1996, more than 1000 potential projects, with an total value of some GBP 27 billion, had been 'identified' in the UK, a veritable bonanza for project finance banks, lawyers, consultants, PR firms, advertising firms, corporate logo

Table 5.2   Industry volume table for US syndicated loans
in 2003

	Total amt (US$ m)	No.
Finance	168 074	247
Utility and power	82 862	184
Oil and gas	73 783	216
Telecommunications	65 376	104
Retail	53 987	154
Healthcare	51 649	190
Real estate	44 768	252
Food and beverage	43 159	111
Insurance	42 061	75
Consumer products	38 372	111
Computers	34 126	114
Automobile	30 289	68
Leisure and recreation	29 951	75
Services	24 942	139
Construction/building	23 839	142
Transportation	23 666	83
Chemicals	19 605	65
Metal and steel	16 927	67
Dining and lodging	16 226	45
Machinery	15 199	50
Publishing	14 542	34
Forestry and paper	13 930	37
Defence and aerospace	11 000	13
Holding companies	9 205	19
Textile	7 677	47
Aerospace/aircraft	6 848	10
Government	5 535	10
Other	4 842	14
Mining	4 841	21
Agribusiness	3 159	15
Unclassified	320	2
Total	980 757	2 712

Source: Dealogic, 2003

designers, specialists and other players. The initiative grew from the idea
that private contractors should not only build infrastructure but also be
responsible for maintaining and servicing it since governments are, in the
PFI *weltanschauungen* it seems, ineffectively and inefficiently staffed.

Table 5.3 Industry volume table for EMEA syndicated loans in 2003

	Total amt (US$ m)	*No.*
Finance	77 660	208
Utility and power	72 070	102
Telecommunications	68 602	60
Transportation	49 086	93
Automobile	45 740	30
Construction/building	38 537	77
Retail	31 436	53
Real estate	30 859	97
Oil and gas	29 084	69
Services	20 993	36
Publishing	19 050	24
Food and beverage	17 174	44
Dining and lodging	16 122	21
Insurance	15 637	19
Chemicals	14 356	38
Metal and steel	14 223	31
Healthcare	13 710	29
Leisure and recreation	12 483	18
Consumer products	11 177	37
Forestry and paper	10 059	19
Mining	8 516	19
Other	8 288	9
Holding companies	7 580	19
Computers	7 224	29
Government	6 256	27
Defence and aerospace	5 236	5
Aerospace/aircraft	3 651	4
Machinery	1 873	11
Textile	1 443	14
Agribusiness	1 350	7
Unclassified	223	2
Total	659 699	1 251

Source: Dealogic, 2003

The thinking was that the subsequent outsourcing of the responsibility to maintain public infrastructure to the private sector would be another welcome reduction in the role of elected governments to provide services in favour of private sector entities whose statutes would specifically

Table 5.4 Industry volume table for Asia–Pacific syndicated loans in 2003

	Total amount (US$ m)	No.
Finance	26 733	121
Computers	19 636	139
Utility and power	17 654	54
Transportation	14 478	94
Real estate	12 208	67
Telecommunications	11 297	48
Holding companies	9575	12
Automobile	9274	32
Construction/building	8553	86
Consumer products	8144	40
Oil and gas	6851	36
Chemicals	6263	46
Metal and steel	5833	35
Food and beverage	5658	43
Retail	5579	52
Services	4792	29
Forestry and paper	4103	18
Healthcare	3591	23
Mining	2671	19
Machinery	2423	41
Government	2264	9
Leisure and recreation	2154	16
Insurance	1988	1
Agribusiness	1633	7
Publishing	1473	9
Textile	1360	22
Dining and lodging	525	9
Other	200	5
Defence and aerospace	49	1
Unclassified	18	1
Aerospace/aircraft	0	0
Total	196 980	1 114

Source: Dealogic, 2003

require them to be run in accordance with profit-driven motives. Thus the scenario arose in which the management of a particular road, hospital, building, railway line or prison might motivate the builder to build it as cheaply as possible, charge the state the maximum for the service and expend the minimal financial resources required to maintain the facility in an effort to maximize profitability and garner favourable stockbroker share recommendations. Whether the state should abdicate its responsibility for the fostering of a transport, health and educational infrastructure in favour of entities whose statutes make it illegal for them to be run on anything other than the profit principle gives rise to concerned debate.

Parties to a typical PFI transaction are:

■ **Treasury**   The Treasury funds PFI projects and its officials are responsible for 'policy developments'.
■ **Private Finance Panel and 4Ps**   PFI for central government projects is promoted by the Private Finance Panel (PFP), a quasi-governmental body funded by the Treasury, and PFI for local authorities by the Public Private Partnership Panel (the 4Ps).
■ **Government agency**   A PFI project can fall under the auspices of either a central government department, a local government body that derives its authority from central government, or a quasi-governmental body such as the National Health Service.
■ **Project company or contractor**   A number of private sector companies will form a consortium and set up a project company or contractor, usually a special purpose vehicle, to tender for the PFI transaction.
■ **Funders**   Most of the funding in UK PFI transactions has come from banks providing loan facilities.

The theory is that, after a period of the contractor managing the asset (so as to gain a return on their capital investment), the asset is returned to the public sector. Most PFI contracts are of long term duration, however, and signed UK projects range from 7 to 99 years, meaning that the problem of managing what will then be ageing and crumbling infrastructure will be well past the time horizon of the elected officials who implemented these schemes, and will thus be someone else's problem.

Appendices

Appendix 1: Generally accepted risk principles risk map

See page 152.

Credit risk	Market risk	Portfolio concentration	Liquidity risk	Operational risk	Business event risk
Direct credit risk	Correlation risk	Instrument	Market liquidity risk	Transaction risk	Currency convertibility
Credit equivalent exposure	Equity risk	Major transaction	Prudential liquidity risk	Execution error	Shift in credit rating
Settlement risk	Equity price risk	Economic sector		Product complexity	Reputation risk
	Equity price volatility risk			Booking error	Taxation risk
	Equity basis risk			Settlement error	Legal risk
	Dividend risk			Commodity delivery risk	Disaster risk
	Interest rate risk			Documentation/contract risk	Natural disasters
	Directional interest rate risk			Operational control risk	War
	Yield curve risk			Exceeding limits	Collapse/suspension of markets
	Interest rate volatility			Rogue trading	Regulatory risk
	Interest rate basis/ spread risk			Fraud	Breaching capital requirements
	Prepayment risk			Money laundering	Regulatory changes
	Currency risk			Security risk	
	FX rate			Key personnel risk	
	FX volatility			Processing risk	
	Profit transition risk			Systems risk	
	Commodity risk			Programming error	
	Commodity price risk			Model/methodology error	
	Forward price risk			Mark-to-market (MTM) error	
	Commodity price volatility risk			Management information	
	Commodity basis/ spread risk			IT systems failure	
	Credit spread risk			Telecommunications failure	
				Contingency planning	

Source: Developed by Coopers & Lybrand

Appendix 2: Credit rating agency rating scales

Moody's issuer rating symbols

Aaa Issuers rated Aaa offer exceptional financial security. While the creditworthiness of these entities is likely to change, such changes as can be visualized are most unlikely to impair their fundamentally strong position

Aa Issuers rated Aa offer excellent financial security. Together with the Aaa group, they constitute what are generally known as high grade entities. They are rated lower than Aaa rated entities because long term risks appear somewhat larger

A Issuers rated A offer good financial security. However elements may be present which suggest a susceptibility to impairment sometime in the future

Baa Issuers rated Baa offer adequate financial security. However, certain protective elements may be lacking or may be unreliable over any great period of time

Ba Issuers rated Ba offer questionable financial security. Often the ability of these entities to meet obligations may be moderate and not well safeguarded in the future

B Issuers rated B offer poor financial security. Assurance of payment of obligations over any long period of time is small

Caa Issuers rated Caa offer very poor financial security. They may be in default on their obligations or there may be present elements of danger with respect to punctual payment of obligations

Ca Issuers rated Ca offer extremely poor financial security. Such entities are often in default on their obligations or have other marked shortcomings

C Issuers rated C are the lowest rated class of entity, are usually in default on their obligations and potential recovery values are low

---

Note: Moody's applies numerical modifiers 1, 2 and 3 in each generic rating category from Aa to Caa. The modifier 1 indicates that the issuer is in the higher end of its letter rating category; the modifier 2 indicates a mid-range ranking; the modifier 3 indicates that the issuer is in the lower end of the letter ranking category.
Source: Moody's Investor Service

Standard & Poor's long term debt ratings

AAA The highest rating assigned by Standard & Poor's. Capacity to pay interest and repay principal is extremely strong

AA A very strong capacity to pay interest and repay principal and differs from the highest rated issues only to a small degree

A Debt rated A has a strong capacity to pay interest and repay principal although it is somewhat more susceptible to the adverse effects of changes in circumstances and economic conditions than debt in higher rated categories

BBB An adequate capacity to pay interest and repay principal. However, adverse economic conditions or changing circumstances are more likely to lead to a weakened capacity to pay interest and repay principal than in higher rated categories

BB Debt rated BB and below is regarded as having predominantly speculative characteristics. The BB rating indicates less near term vulnerability to default than other speculative issues. However, the issuer faces major ongoing uncertainties or exposure to adverse economic conditions which could lead to inadequate capacity to meet timely interest and principal payments

B Indicates a greater vulnerability to default than BB but currently issuer has the capacity to meet interest payments and principal repayments. Adverse business, financial or economic conditions will impair capacity or willingness to pay interest and repay principal

CCC Denotes a currently identifiable vulnerability to default and dependence upon favourable business, financial and economic conditions to meet timely payment of interest and repayment of principal. In the event of adverse business, financial or economic conditions, it is not likely to have the capacity to pay interest and repay principal

CC The rating CC is typically applied to debt subordinated to senior debt that is assigned an actual or implied CC rating

C Typically applied to debt subordinated to senior debt which is assigned an actual or implied CC rating

C1 The rating C1 is reserved for income bonds on which no interest is being paid

D Borrower is in default. The UDU rating is also used when interest payments or principal repayments are expected to be in default at the payment date, and payment of interest and/or repayment or principal is in arrears

---

Note: From AA to Ba + or [−] may be added to give two further gradations of risk for each letter.
Source: Standard & Poor's International Creditweek

Standard & Poor's short term commercial paper debt ratings

A1   The degree of safety regarding timely payment is either overwhelming or very strong. Those issues determined to possess overwhelming safety characteristics are denoted with a plus (+) designation

A2   Capacity for timely payment is strong. However, the relative degree of safety is not as high as for issues rated A1

A3   A satisfactory capacity for timely payment, though somewhat more vulnerable to the adverse effects of changes in circumstances than obligations carrying the higher designations

B   Only an adequate capacity for timely payment. However, such capacity may be damaged by changing conditions or short term adversities

C   Doubtful capacity for payment

D   Issue is either in default or is expected to be in default upon maturity

---

Source: Standard & Poor's International Creditweek

Appendix 3: Country risk criteria

Political risk profile

1 Characteristics of political system
   (a) Type of government
   (b) Process and frequency of political succession
   (c) Degree of public participation
   (d) Degree of centralisation in decision-making process

2 Executive leadership
   (a) Relationship with supporting government institutions
   (b) Relationship with supporting political coalitions

3 Government institutions
   (a) Responsiveness and access to executive leadership
   (b) Effectiveness and efficiency
   (c) Policy responsibilities

4 Social coalitions
   (a) Major socio-economic and cultural groups (i.e., church, military, landowners, management, labour, ethnic groups, etc.)
   (b) Political parties and their constituencies

5 Social indicators
   (a) Level and growth of per capita income, and other measures of the standard of living
   (b) Distribution of wealth and income
   (c) Regional disparities
   (d) Homogeneity of the populace

6 External relations
   (a) Relationship with major trading partners
   (b) Relationship with neighbouring countries
   (c) Participation in international organizations

Economic risk profile

1 Demographic characteristics
   (a) Level and growth of population
   (b) Age distribution
   (c) Urbanization trends

2 Structure of the economy
  (a) Extent and quality of infrastructure
    (i) Transportation and communications
    (ii) Utilities
    (iii) Housing
    (iv) Education
    (v) Health services
  (b) Natural resource endowment
    (i) Agriculture, forestry, fishing
    (ii) Non-energy minerals
    (iii) Energy resources
  (c) Distribution of productive activities
    (i) Agriculture and livestock
      (1) Land tenure system
      (2) Degree of mechanization
      (3) Principal crops
      (4) Markets
    (ii) Forestry and fishing
    (iii) Mining
    (iv) Construction
      (1) Residential
      (2) Non-residential
    (v) Manufacturing
      (1) Concentration and size of manufacturers
      (2) Product types (i.e., consumer, intermediate and capital goods)
      (3) Markets
    (vi) Services-financial/non-financial, public/private
  (d) Public sector participation in productive activities

3 Recent economic trends
  (a) Composition and growth of aggregate demand (nominal and real terms)
    (i) Consumption
      (1) Private sector
      (2) Public sector

      (ii) Investment

          (1) Private sector

          (2) Public sector

    (iii) External savings (i.e., exports/imports)

  (b) Domestic economy

      (i) Total production (i.e. GDP)

     (ii) Production by sector

          (1) Agriculture, forestry and fishing

          (2) Mining

          (3) Construction

          (4) Manufacturing

          (5) Utilities

          (6) Services

    (iii) Price movements and major determinants

          (1) External factors

          (2) Wages

          (3) Public sector deficit financing

          (4) Private sector credit expansion

          (5) Supply bottlenecks

    (iv) Employment trends

          (1) Level of growth of employment and labour force

          (2) Labour participation rates

          (3) Unemployment rate and structure

          (4) Sectorial trends

          (5) Regional trends

          (6) Composition of employment: public *vs.* private

  (c) External sector

      (i) Current account balance

          (1) Export growth and composition

              (a) Agricultural commodities

              (b) Minerals

              (c) Manufactured goods

          (2) Destination of exports (i.e. markets)

          (3) Price and income elasticity of exports

          (4) Import growth and composition

              (a) Food

              (b) Other consumer goods

      (c) Energy

      (d) Other intermediate goods

      (e) Capital goods

   (5) Price and income elasticity of imports

   (6) Geographic origin of imports

   (7) Terms of trade

   (8) Services account

      (a) Interest payments and receipts

      (b) Transportation

      (c) Other

   (9) Transfers

(ii) Capital account balance

   (1) Direct investment

   (2) Long term capital flows

      (a) Private sector

      (b) Public sector

   (3) Shortterm capital flows

   (4) Access to capital markets

      (a) Types of instruments used

      (b) Types of borrowers and lenders

(iii) International reserves

   (1) Level

   (2) Composition (i.e. gold, foreign exchange)

   (3) Secondary reserves

(iv) External debt

   (1) Amount outstanding

   (2) Composition by borrower

      (a) Central government

      (b) Other public sector

      (c) Publicly guaranteed

      (d) Private

   (3) Composition by lender

      (a) Bilateral

      (b) Multilateral

      (c) Private financial institutions

      (d) Suppliers' credits

   (4) Maturity structure

(5) Currency composition

(6) Growth rate

(7) Comparison with export earnings and GDP

(8) Debt service payments

(a) Amortization

(b) Interest

(c) Comparison with export earnings

(d) Future debt service schedule

4 Economic policy

(a) Price and wage policies

(i) Wage settlement process

(1) Trade union activity

(2) Management groups

(3) Role and influence of government

(ii) Degree of wage indexation

(iii) Productivity trends

(iv) Non-wage benefits and unemployment insurance

(v) Direct price controls

(1) Public sector tariffs

(2) Private sector pricing

(vi) Price subsidies (agricultural, industrial, etc.)

(b) Monetary policy

(i) Level of development of financial system

(1) Types of financial institutions

(2) Types of financial instruments

(3) Role of government in credit allocation

(4) Foreign participation

(ii) Trends for monetary aggregates

(1) Money supply growth targets and actual experience

(2) Domestic credit expansion

(a) Public sector

(b) Private sector

(3) Velocity (national income/money supply)

(4) Changes in international reserves

(iii) Monetary policy instruments

(1) Reserve requirements

(2) Open market operations

        (3) Credit controls

        (4) Interest rate regulations

        (5) Ability to sterilize international reserve flows

        (6) Controls on foreign borrowing

        (7) Rediscount facilities

(c) Fiscal policy

    (i) Structure of the public sector

        (1) Central government

        (2) Social security system

        (3) State agencies and enterprises

        (4) Regional and local governments

    (ii) Budgetary process

        (1) Executive branch

        (2) Legislative branch

        (3) Major constituencies (business, labour, etc.)

    (iii) Revenues

        (1) Composition

            (a) Direct taxes – personal income, corporate income, property, others

            (b) Indirect taxes – valued added, sales, export and import duties, others

            (c) Service charges and public sector tariffs

        (2) Income elasticity of revenues

        (3) Distribution of tax burden by income groups

        (4) Overall tax burden (% of GDP)

        (5) Tax collection and evasion

        (6) Tax incentives (i.e., investment, export, employment)

    (iv) Expenditures

        (1) Current expenditures

            (a) Distribution by expenditure category

            (b) Transfers to households

            (c) Transfers to other levels of government

        (2) Capital expenditures

    (v) Current operating balance (absolute level and relative to GDP)

    (vi) Gross financing requirements (operating balance plus net capital expenditures)

        (1) Trend relative to GDP

          (2) Means of financing
             (a) Domestic money creation
             (b) Domestic borrowing
             (c) External borrowing
      (vii) Public sector debt: domestic and external
          (1) Size (direct and guaranteed)
          (2) Debt service requirement
          (3) Debt management
  (d) External policies
      (i) Exchange rate policy
     (ii) International reserve management
    (iii) Export promotion measures
    (iv) Import substitution/trade protectionist measures
  (e) Long term planning and special programmes
      (i) Energy
     (ii) Industrial development/restructuring
    (iii) Employment creation
    (iv) Others

S&P's sovereign rating profile

In order to evaluate the elements in the preceding political and economic risk profile, the most recent five years of the following information should be incorporated.

Demographic characteristics
  (a) Total population (millions)
  (b) Age structure (% of total)
      (i) 0–14
     (ii) 15–64
    (iii) 66 and over
  (c) Urban population (% of total)
  (d) Total labour force (millions)
      (i) % Employment agriculture
     (ii) % Employment industry
Economic structure and growth
  (a) GDP, current prices
  (b) GDP, constant prices

 (c) GDP per capita, current prices

 (d) Composition of real GDP (%)

   (i) Agriculture

   (ii) Mining

   (iii) Manufacturing

   (iv) Construction

   (v) Electricity, gas and water

   (vi) Transportation and communication

   (vii) Trade and finance

   (viii) Public administration

   (ix) Other services

 (e) Investment, constant prices

 (f) Investment, current prices

 (g) Investment/GDP

 (h) Net energy imports/total energy consumption (%)

Economic management

 (a) Consumer price index

 (b) Money supply M1

 (c) Money supply M2

 (d) Domestic credit

 (e) Wage index

 (f) Unemployment rate

 (g) Budget deficit/GDP (%)

 (h) Public expenditures/GDP (%)

Government finance

 (a) Current revenues

 (b) Current expenditures

 (c) Operating balance

 (d) Net capital expenditures

 (e) Budgetary balance

 (f) Non-budgetary balance

 (g) Domestic financing

 (h) Foreign financing

External payments

 (a) Exchange rate

   (i) Local currency/USUSD

   (ii) Local currency/SDR

(b) Imports/GDP (%)
(c) Composition of imports (%)
    (i) Food
    (ii) Non-food agricultural
    (iii) Non-fuel mining and metals
    (iv) Fuels
    (v) Machinery and equipment
    (vi) Other manufactured goods
(d) Composition of exports (%)
    (i) Food
    (ii) Non-food agricultural
    (iii) Non-fuel mining and metals
    (iv) Fuels
    (v) Machinery and equipment
    (vi) Other manufactured goods
(e) Balance of payments
    (i) Exports
    (ii) Imports
    (iii) Trade balance
    (iv) Net factor services (interest payments)
    (v) Net transfers
    (vi) Current account balance
    (vii) Long term capital flows
        (1) Public
        (2) Private
    (viii) Short term capital flows
        (1) Public
        (2) Private
    (ix) Errors and omissions
    (x) Reserves movements
    (xi) Current account balance/GDP (%)
    (xii) Current account balance/exports (%)
(f) International reserves
    (i) Central bank reserves, minus gold
    (ii) Central bank gold reserves (millions of troy ounces)
    (iii) Reserves, rest of banking system
    (iv) Reserves/imports (%)

      (v) Net foreign assets of banking system
      (vi) Imports (%)

(g) External Debt
      (i) Long term debt
          (1) Public
          (2) Private
      (ii) Short term debt
          (1) Public
          (2) Private
      (iii) External debt/GDP (%)
      (iv) Debt service payments
          (1) Public
          (2) Private
      (v) Debt service payments/exports (%)
      (vi) Debt service schedule

Appendix 4: World Bank country categories

http://www.worldbank.org/data/databytopic/CLASS.XLS

	Economy	Region	Income group	Indebtedness
1	Afghanistan	South Asia	Low	Severely indebted
2	Albania	Europe & Central Asia	Lower Mid	Less indebted
3	Algeria	Mid East & N Africa	Lower Mid	Less indebted
4	American Samoa	East Asia & Pacific	Upper Mid	Debt not classified
5	Andorra		High: non-OECD	Debt not classified
6	Angola	Sub-Saharan Africa	Low	Severely indebted
7	Antigua and Barbuda	Latin America & Carib	Upper Mid	Less indebted
8	Argentina	Latin America & Carib	Upper Mid	Severely indebted
9	Armenia	Europe & Central Asia	Low	Less indebted
10	Aruba		High: non-OECD	Debt not classified
11	Australia		High: OECD	Debt not classified
12	Austria		High: OECD	Debt not classified
13	Azerbaijan	Europe & Central Asia	Low	Less indebted
14	Bahamas, The		High: non-OECD	Debt not classified
15	Bahrain		High: non-OECD	Debt not classified
16	Bangladesh	South Asia	Low	Less indebted
17	Barbados	Latin America & Carib	Upper Mid	Less indebted
18	Belarus	Europe & Central Asia	Lower Mid	Less indebted
19	Belgium		High: OECD	Debt not classified
20	Belize	Latin America & Carib	Lower Mid	Severely indebted
21	Benin	Sub-Saharan Africa	Low	Severely indebted
22	Bermuda		High: non-OECD	Debt not classified
23	Bhutan	South Asia	Low	Moderately indebted
24	Bolivia	Latin America & Carib	Lower Mid	Moderately indebted
25	Bosnia and Herzegovina	Europe & Central Asia	Lower Mid	Less indebted
26	Botswana	Sub-Saharan Africa	Upper Mid	Less indebted

(continued)

	Economy	Region	Income group	Indebtedness
27	Brazil	Latin America & Carib	Upper Mid	Severely indebted
28	Brunei		High: non-OECD	Debt not classified
29	Bulgaria	Europe & Central Asia	Lower Mid	Moderately indebted
30	Burkina Faso	Sub-Saharan Africa	Low	Severely indebted
31	Burundi	Sub-Saharan Africa	Low	Severely indebted
32	Cambodia	East Asia & Pacific	Low	Moderately indebted
33	Cameroon	Sub-Saharan Africa	Low	Moderately indebted
34	Canada		High: OECD	Debt not classified
35	Cape Verde	Sub-Saharan Africa	Lower Mid	Less indebted
36	Cayman Islands		High: non-OECD	Debt not classified
37	Central African Republic	Sub-Saharan Africa	Low	Severely indebted
38	Chad	Sub-Saharan Africa	Low	Severely indebted
39	Channel Islands		High: non-OECD	Debt not classified
40	Chile	Latin America & Carib	Upper Mid	Moderately indebted
41	China	East Asia & Pacific	Lower Mid	Less indebted
42	Colombia	Latin America & Carib	Lower Mid	Moderately indebted
43	Comoros	Sub-Saharan Africa	Low	Severely indebted
44	Congo, Dem. Rep.	Sub-Saharan Africa	Low	Severely indebted
45	Congo, Rep.	Sub-Saharan Africa	Low	Severely indebted
46	Costa Rica	Latin America & Carib	Upper Mid	Less indebted
47	Côte d'Ivoire	Sub-Saharan Africa	Low	Severely indebted
48	Croatia	Europe & Central Asia	Upper Mid	Moderately indebted
49	Cuba	Latin America & Carib	Lower Mid	Severely indebted
50	Cyprus		High: non-OECD	Debt not classified

(continued)

	Economy	Region	Income group	Indebtedness
51	Czech Republic	Europe & Central Asia	Upper Mid	Less indebted
52	Denmark		High: OECD	Debt not classified
53	Djibouti	Mid East & N Africa	Lower Mid	Less indebted
54	Dominica	Latin America & Carib	Upper Mid	Moderately indebted
55	Dominican Republic	Latin America & Carib	Lower Mid	Less indebted
56	Ecuador	Latin America & Carib	Lower Mid	Severely indebted
57	Egypt, Arab Rep.	Mid East & N Africa	Lower Mid	Less indebted
58	El Salvador	Latin America & Carib	Lower Mid	Less indebted
59	Equatorial Guinea	Sub-Saharan Africa	Low	Less indebted
60	Eritrea	Sub-Saharan Africa	Low	Less indebted
61	Estonia	Europe & Central Asia	Upper Mid	Moderately indebted
62	Ethiopia	Sub-Saharan Africa	Low	Severely indebted
63	Faeroe Islands		High: non-OECD	Debt not classified
64	Fiji	East Asia & Pacific	Lower Mid	Less indebted
65	Finland		High: OECD	Debt not classified
66	France		High: OECD	Debt not classified
67	French Polynesia		High: non-OECD	Debt not classified
68	Gabon	Sub-Saharan Africa	Upper Mid	Severely indebted
69	Gambia, The	Sub-Saharan Africa	Low	Severely indebted
70	Georgia	Europe & Central Asia	Low	Less indebted
71	Germany		High: OECD	Debt not classified
72	Ghana	Sub-Saharan Africa	Low	Moderately indebted
73	Greece		High: OECD	Debt not classified
74	Greenland		High: non-OECD	Debt not classified
75	Grenada	Latin America & Carib	Upper Mid	Moderately indebted
76	Guam		High: non-OECD	Debt not classified
77	Guatemala	Latin America & Carib	Lower Mid	Less indebted

(continued)

	Economy	Region	Income group	Indebtedness
78	Guinea	Sub-Saharan Africa	Low	Severely indebted
79	Guinea-Bissau	Sub-Saharan Africa	Low	Severely indebted
80	Guyana	Latin America & Carib	Lower Mid	Severely indebted
81	Haiti	Latin America & Carib	Low	Moderately indebted
82	Honduras	Latin America & Carib	Lower Mid	Moderately indebted
83	Hong Kong, China		High: non-OECD	Debt not classified
84	Hungary	Europe & Central Asia	Upper Mid	Moderately indebted
85	Iceland		High: OECD	Debt not classified
86	India	South Asia	Low	Less indebted
87	Indonesia	East Asia & Pacific	Low	Severely indebted
88	Iran, Islamic Rep.	Mid East & N Africa	Lower Mid	Less indebted
89	Iraq	Mid East & N Africa	Lower Mid	Severely indebted
90	Ireland		High: OECD	Debt not classified
91	Isle of Man	Europe & Central Asia	Upper Mid	Debt not classified
92	Israel		High: non-OECD	Debt not classified
93	Italy		High: OECD	Debt not classified
94	Jamaica	Latin America & Carib	Lower Mid	Moderately indebted
95	Japan		High: OECD	Debt not classified
96	Jordan	Mid East & N Africa	Lower Mid	Severely indebted
97	Kazakhstan	Europe & Central Asia	Lower Mid	Moderately indebted
98	Kenya	Sub-Saharan Africa	Low	Moderately indebted
99	Kiribati	East Asia & Pacific	Lower Mid	Less indebted
100	Korea, Dem. Rep.	East Asia & Pacific	Low	Less indebted
101	Korea, Rep.		High: OECD	Debt not classified
102	Kuwait		High: non-OECD	Debt not classified
103	Kyrgyz Republic	Europe & Central Asia	Low	Severely indebted
104	Lao PDR	East Asia & Pacific	Low	Severely indebted

(continued)

	Economy	Region	Income group	Indebtedness
105	Latvia	Europe & Central Asia	Upper Mid	Moderately indebted
106	Lebanon	Mid East & N Africa	Upper Mid	Severely indebted
107	Lesotho	Sub-Saharan Africa	Low	Less indebted
108	Liberia	Sub-Saharan Africa	Low	Severely indebted
109	Libya	Mid East & N Africa	Upper Mid	Less indebted
110	Liechtenstein		High: non-OECD	Debt not classified
111	Lithuania	Europe & Central Asia	Upper Mid	Less indebted
112	Luxembourg		High: OECD	Debt not classified
113	Macao, China		High: non-OECD	Debt not classified
114	Macedonia, FYR	Europe & Central Asia	Lower Mid	Less indebted
115	Madagascar	Sub-Saharan Africa	Low	Severely indebted
116	Malawi	Sub-Saharan Africa	Low	Severely indebted
117	Malaysia	East Asia & Pacific	Upper Mid	Moderately indebted
118	Maldives	South Asia	Lower Mid	Less indebted
119	Mali	Sub-Saharan Africa	Low	Moderately indebted
120	Malta	Mid East & N Africa	Upper Mid	Less indebted
121	Marshall Islands	East Asia & Pacific	Lower Mid	Debt not classified
122	Mauritania	Sub-Saharan Africa	Low	Severely indebted
123	Mauritius	Sub-Saharan Africa	Upper Mid	Less indebted
124	Mayotte	Sub-Saharan Africa	Upper Mid	Debt not classified
125	Mexico	Latin America & Carib	Upper Mid	Less indebted
126	Micronesia, Fed. Sts.	East Asia & Pacific	Lower Mid	Debt not classified
127	Moldova	Europe & Central Asia	Low	Severely indebted
128	Monaco		High: non-OECD	Debt not classified
129	Mongolia	East Asia & Pacific	Low	Moderately indebted
130	Morocco	Mid East & N Africa	Lower Mid	Less indebted

(continued)

	Economy	Region	Income group	Indebtedness
131	Mozambique	Sub-Saharan Africa	Low	Less indebted
132	Myanmar	East Asia & Pacific	Low	Severely indebted
133	Namibia	Sub-Saharan Africa	Lower Mid	Less indebted
134	Nepal	South Asia	Low	Less indebted
135	Netherlands		High: OECD	Debt not classified
136	Netherlands Antilles		High: non-OECD	Debt not classified
137	New Caledonia		High: non-OECD	Debt not classified
138	New Zealand		High: OECD	Debt not classified
139	Nicaragua	Latin America & Carib	Low	Severely indebted
140	Niger	Sub-Saharan Africa	Low	Severely indebted
141	Nigeria	Sub-Saharan Africa	Low	Severely indebted
142	Northern Mariana Islands		High: non-OECD	Debt not classified
143	Norway		High: OECD	Debt not classified
144	Oman	Mid East & N Africa	Upper Mid	Less indebted
145	Pakistan	South Asia	Low	Severely indebted
146	Palau	East Asia & Pacific	Upper Mid	Debt not classified
147	Panama	Latin America & Carib	Upper Mid	Severely indebted
148	Papua New Guinea	East Asia & Pacific	Low	Moderately indebted
149	Paraguay	Latin America & Carib	Lower Mid	Less indebted
150	Peru	Latin America & Carib	Lower Mid	Severely indebted
151	Philippines	East Asia & Pacific	Lower Mid	Moderately indebted
152	Poland	Europe & Central Asia	Upper Mid	Less indebted
153	Portugal		High: OECD	Debt not classified
154	Puerto Rico	Latin America & Carib	Upper Mid	Debt not classified
155	Qatar		High: non-OECD	Debt not classified
156	Romania	Europe & Central Asia	Lower Mid	Less indebted
157	Russian Federation	Europe & Central Asia	Lower Mid	Moderately indebted

(*continued*)

	Economy	*Region*	*Income group*	*Indebtedness*
158	Rwanda	Sub-Saharan Africa	Low	Severely indebted
159	Samoa	East Asia & Pacific	Lower Mid	Moderately indebted
160	San Marino		High: non-OECD	Debt not classified
161	São Tomé and Principe	Sub-Saharan Africa	Low	Severely indebted
162	Saudi Arabia	Mid East & N Africa	Upper Mid	Less indebted
163	Senegal	Sub-Saharan Africa	Low	Moderately indebted
164	Seychelles	Sub-Saharan Africa	Upper Mid	Less indebted
165	Sierra Leone	Sub-Saharan Africa	Low	Severely indebted
166	Singapore		High: non-OECD	Debt not classified
167	Slovak Republic	Europe & Central Asia	Upper Mid	Moderately indebted
168	Slovenia		High: non-OECD	Debt not classified
169	Solomon Islands	East Asia & Pacific	Low	Less indebted
170	Somalia	Sub-Saharan Africa	Low	Severely indebted
171	South Africa	Sub-Saharan Africa	Lower Mid	Less indebted
172	Spain		High: OECD	Debt not classified
173	Sri Lanka	South Asia	Lower Mid	Less indebted
174	St. Kitts and Nevis	Latin America & Carib	Upper Mid	Moderately indebted
175	St. Lucia	Latin America & Carib	Upper Mid	Less indebted
176	St. Vin Central Grenadines	Latin America & Carib	Lower Mid	Moderately indebted
177	Sudan	Sub-Saharan Africa	Low	Severely indebted
178	Suriname	Latin America & Carib	Lower Mid	Less indebted
179	Swaziland	Sub-Saharan Africa	Lower Mid	Less indebted
180	Sweden		High: OECD	Debt not classified
181	Switzerland		High: OECD	Debt not classified
182	Syrian Arab Republic	Mid East & N Africa	Lower Mid	Severely indebted
183	Tajikistan	Europe & Central Asia	Low	Severely indebted
184	Tanzania	Sub-Saharan Africa	Low	Moderately indebted

(continued)

	Economy	Region	Income group	Indebtedness
185	Thailand	East Asia & Pacific	Lower Mid	Moderately indebted
186	Timor-Leste	East Asia & Pacific	Low	Debt not classified
187	Togo	Sub-Saharan Africa	Low	Moderately indebted
188	Tonga	East Asia & Pacific	Lower Mid	Less indebted
189	Trinidad and Tobago	Latin America & Carib	Upper Mid	Less indebted
190	Tunisia	Mid East & N Africa	Lower Mid	Moderately indebted
191	Turkey	Europe & Central Asia	Lower Mid	Moderately indebted
192	Turkmenistan	Europe & Central Asia	Lower Mid	Moderately indebted
193	Uganda	Sub-Saharan Africa	Low	Moderately indebted
194	Ukraine	Europe & Central Asia	Low	Less indebted
195	United Arab Emirates		High: non-OECD	Debt not classified
196	United Kingdom		High: OECD	Debt not classified
197	United States		High: OECD	Debt not classified
198	Uruguay	Latin America & Carib	Upper Mid	Severely indebted
199	Uzbekistan	Europe & Central Asia	Low	Moderately indebted
200	Vanuatu	East Asia & Pacific	Lower Mid	Less indebted
201	Venezuela, RB	Latin America & Carib	Upper Mid	Less indebted
202	Vietnam	East Asia & Pacific	Low	Less indebted
203	Virgin Islands (U.S.)		High: non-OECD	Debt not classified
204	West Bank and Gaza	Mid East & N Africa	Lower Mid	Debt not classified
205	Yemen, Rep.	Mid East & N Africa	Low	Less indebted
206	Yugoslavia, Fed. Rep.	Europe & Central Asia	Lower Mid	Severely indebted
207	Zambia	Sub-Saharan Africa	Low	Severely indebted
208	Zimbabwe	Sub-Saharan Africa	Low	Moderately indebted

(continued)

1 World
2 Low income	LIC
3 Middle income	MIC
4 Lower middle income	LMC
5 Upper middle income	UMC
6 Low & middle income	LMY
7 East Asia & Pacific	EAP
8 Europe & Central Asia	ECA
9 Latin America & Caribbean	LAC
10 Middle East & North Africa	MNA
11 South Asia	SAS
12 Sub-Saharan Africa	SSA
13 High income	HIC
14 European Monetary Union	EMU
15 High income: OECD	OEC
16 High income: non-OECD	NOC
17 Heavily indebted poor (HIPC)	HPC
18 Least developed countries	LDC

Glossary

Acceleration   After a default, the loan is fully due and payable. Repayments are accelerated to the present.

Account party   In a commercial letter of credit, the party instructing the bank to open a letter of credit and on whose behalf the bank agrees to make payment.

Accrued interest   Interest earned but not collected.

Acid test or quick ratio   Current assets, less inventories divided by current liabilities.

Ad valorem   Off the gross or stated value, usually a percentage.

ADB   Asian Development Bank.

Advance agent   A loan drawdown is advanced by the funder.

After tax cash flow   Total cash generated by the project annually, defined as profit after tax plus depreciation.

Agent   The bank charged with administering the project financing. Generic: a party appointed to act on behalf of a principal entity/ person.

All-in rate   Interest rate which includes margin, commitment fees, up-front fees.

Amortisation   The process of paying off an amount gradually by spreading the payments over several years.

Annual report   The company's annual accounts, audit statements and narrative account of the year at hand. Presentations vary considerably.

Annuity   The sum of principal and interest is equal for each period.

Arbitrage   Take advantage of discrepancies in price or yields in different markets.

Arranger   The senior tier of a syndication. This implies the entity that agreed and negotiated the project finance structure. Also refers to the bank/underwriter entitled to syndicate the loan/bond issue.

Asset   The physical project and its associated contracts, rights and interests of every kind, in the present or future, which can be valued or used to repay debt.

Asset turnover ratio   A broad measure of asset efficiency, defined as net sales divided by total assets.

Asset-backed securities   Securities collateralized by a pool of assets. The process of creating securities backed by assets is referred to as asset securitization.

Assets   Any item owned by a company or individual that can be given a monetary value and used if necessary to pay debts. There are many kinds of assets, described by terms like current assets and fixed assets.

Assignment   Grant of the right to step in to the position of a party to a contract or legal agreement.

Audit   An official examination and checking of a company's accounts by an independent accountant called an auditor, to certify that the accounts (as presented by the directors) comply with the law, and in their opinion give a true and fair view of the company's affairs.

Auditors   Accountants who certify that the company's accounts have been reviewed in accordance with FRS (Financial Reporting Standards for the UK – see below) and note the findings of their inquiry.

Authorized signatories   Persons authorized to sign on behalf of the company borrowing the money. Specimen signatures are usually in a booklet provided by the company. It is the bank's (i.e. analyst's) responsibility to verify this: if the signatory is not authorized, the company does not have to pay the money back.

Availability   The project financing is available for drawdown. A period prior to financial close may also be included.

Available cash flow   Total cash sources less total cash uses before payment of debt service.

Average life   Average for all repayments, usually weighted by amounts outstanding.

Avoided cost   The capital and expense that would otherwise have to be spent if the project did not proceed.

Balance sheet   The accounts which show assets, liabilities, net worth/ shareholders' equity.

Balloon payment   A large single repayment.

Barter   The physical form of countertrade.

Basis point (bp)   One hundred bp equals 1 percentage point.

Bearer bond   The bond certificate is itself negotiable. (It is not recorded as being owned by any particular Investor.)

Best efforts   A very high standard of undertaking, nevertheless excusable in the event of force majeure or failure to execute the matter in question after trying to do so on a sustained, dedicated basis.

BI   Business interruption insurance available once the project is in business.

Bid bond   A small percentage (1–3%) of the tender contract price is established as a bid 'performance' bond. Once the contract is awarded, bid bonds are refunded to the losers.

Blocked currency   Due to inconvertibility or transfer risk, a currency cannot be moved out of the country.

Bond   The paper evidence of a legal promise by the issuer to pay the investor on the declared terms. Bonds are usually negotiable. Bonds are customarily longer term, say 5–25 years. Short term bonds are usually referred to as notes.

BOO   Build Own Operate (and Maintain).

Book runner   The arranger or bank extending the invitations for a syndication and tallying final take.

Borrower risk   Risks pertaining to the company, including management, profitability, non-performance and bankruptcy: all factors relating to the borrower.

BOT   Build Own Transfer where the project is transferred back to the party granting the concession. The transfer may be for value or at no cost.

Break even   The reduction of a project finance net cash flow to zero by changing an input variable such as price or costs.

Broker   A party which brings together sponsors, finance or insurances but is not acting as a principal.

Builders All Risk   The standard insurance package during construction.

Bullet repayment   A loan whose interest is payable at intervals agreed in the loan agreement, and whose principal is repayable in a lump sum at final maturity. The source of repayment is usually a new facility that is put into place.

Buy-back   A promise to repurchase unsold production. Alternatively, a promise to repay a financial obligation.

Buydown   A once-off payment out of LDs to reflect cash flow losses from sustained underperformance. Often used to 'buy' down the project finance loan.

Buyer credit   A financing provided to a buyer to pay for the supply of goods or services usually by an exporting country or the supplier company.

Call   An option to buy a security or commodity for a set price at a given time in the future.

Call option   A contract sold for a price that gives the holder the right to buy from the writer of the option, over a specified period, a specified property or amount of securities at a specified price.

Cap   A ceiling on an interest or FX rate through a swap, options, or by agreement.

Capex   Capital expenditures, usually by way of direct investment.

Capital markets   A broad term to include tradable debt, securities and equity as distinct from private markets or banks.

Capitalized interest   Prior to completion, the convention is to capitalize interest into the project financing, i.e. to borrow to pay Interest. See IDC.

Cash flow   The generation of cash by a project.

CDC   Commonwealth Development Corp., a British development finance institute.

Certificates of registration   These certify that the company has registered with the state authorities. Photocopies are usually available from the company on request.

Charge   Under Crown Law, the document evidencing mortgage security. A fixed charge refers to a defined set of assets and is usually registered. A floating charge refers to other assets which change from time to time, e.g. cash at bank, inventory, etc., which become a fixed charge after a default.

Claw back   The ability to recover prior project cash flow that may have been distributed/paid away as dividends to the sponsors.

Club   A group of underwriters who do not need to proceed to syndication.

Coface   The French ECA.

Co-financing   Where the different lenders agree to fund under the same documentation and security packages yet may have different interest rates, repayment profiles and term, perhaps via A and B tranches.

Collar   A ceiling and floor to an interest or FX rate structured through swaps, options, hedging, or by agreement.

Collateral   Additional security pledged to support a project financing.

Collateral   See Security.

Co-Manager   A second-tier participant, ranked by size of participation.

Commitment fee   A per annum fee applied to the portion of the unused project financing (the amount not yet drawn down) until the end of the availability period.

Compensation trade   The form of countertrade where an incoming investment is repaid from the units/revenues generated by that investment.

Complementary financing   Where different lenders agree to fund under similar yet parallel documentation and a pro-rata security package.

Completion   In a project financing, when the project's cash flows become the primary method of repayment. It occurs after a completion test. Prior to completion, the primary source of repayment is usually from the sponsors or from the turnkey contractor.

Completion risk   Construction, development, or cost overrun risk. The risk that a project will not be able to pass its completion test.

Completion test   A test of the project's ability to perform as planned and generate the expected cash flows. The time when the project can move from recourse to a project financing.

Compound   Interest is reinvested to earn additional interest in the following period.

Consortium   All of the participants or developers. For the early stages of a project, it may be a loose association, not a legal or contractual entity/JV.

Constant dollar   Inflation or escalation is not applicable. Prices and costs are de-escalated/re-escalated to a single point in time.

Contingency   An additional amount/percentage to any cash flow item. e.g. Capex. Care is needed to ensure it is either 'to-be-spent' or a cushion.

Contingent liabilities   Items that do not represent a liability on the balance sheet at the time of statement date but which could do so in the future. Such items include guarantees issued in favour of third parties, and lawsuits currently in progress whose outcome is uncertain.

Convertible   A financial instrument that can be exchanged for another security or equity interest at a pre-agreed time and exchange ratio.

Counterparty   The other participant, usually in a swap or contract and includes intermediaries.

Countertrade   One party supplies a unit/funding in return for other material/funding. See Barter.

Country risk   Includes sovereign risk but usually an estimate of the likelihood of a country debt rescheduling which will prompt currency Inconvertibility. Sometimes referred to as sovereign risk.

Coupon   The interest amount or rate payable on a bond. A coupon may be physically attached to the bond certificate.

Covenants   Conditions in the loan agreement signed by the bank and the borrower which the borrower must respect. Covenants can cover conditions on management performance, disposal of subsidiaries, negative pledges, amounts of debt incurred and adherence to financial ratios. Non-compliance is known as an event of default.

Cover   The amount above unity of a debt service ratio.

CPI   Consumer Price Index, a measure of inflation at the consumer level.

Credit enhancement   The issuance of a guarantee, L/Q or additional collateral to reinforce the credit strength of a project financing.

Credit scoring   Technique used to evaluate a potential borrower according to a pre-defined matrix procedure. Usually used in retail banking and credit card processing, may be used in evaluating corporates.

Creditworthy   The risk of default on a debt obligation by that entity is deemed low.

Cross default   A default by another project participant or by the sponsor (other than the project financing) triggers a default.

Cross-collateral   Project participants agree to pool collateral, i.e. allow recourse to each other's collateral.

Crown Law   Law derived from English law, e.g. England, Ireland, Canada, Australia, Papua–New Guinea, Hong Kong, Singapore, India, Malaysia.

Cure   Make good a default.

Current asset   Cash or assets that can be converted to cash within one year.

Current dollar   Actual or real prices and costs. Escalation/inflation effects are included.

Current liabilities   Liabilities payable within one year.

Current ratio   Current assets divided by current liabilities (a liquidity ratio).

Cushion   The extra amount of net cash flow remaining after expected debt service.

D:E ratio   The amount of debt as a ratio of equity, often expressed as a percentage.

D:E swap   Debt in a blocked currency is swapped for equity in a local company project, usually at a discount.

DCF   Discounted cash flow where net cash flow is brought to a present value using a given percentage discount rate.

Debenture   A legal security over the Issuer's general credit/balance sheet.

Debottle-necking   Each transition of a project's flowsheet or sequence is optimized to increase output. This may require minimal Capex.

Debt   The obligation to repay an agreed amount of money.

Debt service   Principal repayments plus interest payable; usually expressed as the annual dollar/currency amount per calendar or financial year.

Deductible   An amount or period which must be deducted before an insurance payout or settlement is calculated.

Default   A covenant has been broken or an adverse event has occurred. A money default means a repayment was not made on time. A technical default means a project parameter is outside defined/agreed limits or a legal matter is not yet resolved.

Default interest   A higher interest rate payable after default.

Defeasance   Some or all of the debt is cash collateralized usually indirectly or via zero-coupon structures.

Deficiency   The amount by which project cash flow is not adequate for debt service.

Deficiency agreement   Where cash flow, working capital or revenues are below agreed levels or are insufficient to meet debt service, then a deficiency or make-up agreement provides the shortfall to be provided by the sponsor or another party, sometimes to a cumulative limit.

Defined event   The definition applicable to the trigger of a loss in an insurance policy, particularly PRI.

Depreciation   Amortization for accounting (book), tax calculations, or income calculations. A regular reduction in asset value over time.

Derivative   A financial instrument based on an underlying contract or funding such as a swap, option or hedge.

Devaluation   Either a formal reduction in the FX rate or gradually according to FX market forces.

DIS   Delay-in-start-up insurances which can cover all non-site forces majeures, change in a law and contingent contractor liability (efficacy). Sometimes called advanced loss-of-profits insurances or advanced business interruption insurance.

Discount rate   The annual percentage applied to NPV or PV calculations (and is often the all-in interest rate or the interest rate plus margin for project financing). The discount rate may be the WACC.

Dividend   The amount paid out per share, usually once or twice a year, by a company from its profits as decided by the board of directors.

Documentation   Anything (such as certificates of registration, loan agreements, guarantees, etc.) relating to the legal agreements and guarantees governing the facility extended to the borrower.

Documentation risk   The risk of non-repayment due to a defect in the loan agreement or security arrangements. This can arise due to faulty drafting, mitigating circumstances, juridically non-enforceable and faulty collateral, or guarantees which have expired and not been renewed. The analyst is not expected to assess legal issues, but is expected to obtain legal opinions when necessary and note them in the credit analysis.

Double dip   Tax depreciation is accessed in two countries concurrently.

Drawdown   The borrower obtains some of the project financing, usually progressively according to construction expenditures plus IDC.

Drop-dead   A fee payable when the underlying transaction does not proceed.

DSCR   Debt service cover ratio; usually annual.

DTI   Department of Trade and Industry. It is a valuable source of information on companies and many business matters in the UK and abroad.

Earnings   Net income, net profit.

EBIT   Earnings before interest and taxes.

EBIT DA   Earnings before interest and tax, depreciation and amortization.

EBRD   European Bank for Reconstruction and Development targeted at Eastern Europe and the former Soviet Union, an MIA.

ECA   Export Credit Agency established by a country to finance its national's goods, investment, and services. They often offer PRI.

ECGD   Export Credit Guarantee Department, the UK ECA.

EDC   Export Development Corp., Canada's ECA.

EFIC   Export Finance Insurance Corp., Australia's ECA.

EIS   Environmental Impact Statement, which may have been subject to public comment.

Engineering risk   Design risk. The impact on project cash flow from deficiencies in design or engineering.

Environmental risk   Economic or administrative consequence of slow or catastrophic environmental pollution.

Equity   In a project financing, the cash or assets contributed by the sponsors. For accounting, it is the net worth or total assets minus liabilities. In the context of credit analysis, this refers to the net value of all assets after deduction of all charges. Also known as share capital or shareholder's funds.

Equity kicker   A share of ownership interest in a company, project or property, or a potential ownership in them. The kicker may take the form of stock, warrants, purchase options, percentage of profits, or percentage of ownership.

Escrow   Where documents or money accounts are put beyond the reach of the parties.

Eurobonds   Bonds issued in any currency and are commonly listed in Luxembourg. They cannot be traded in the USA. Eurobonds are often bearer bonds.

Eurodollar   US$ deposited with banks outside the USA.

Events of default   A pledge in the loan agreement which the borrower fails to meet, enabling the bank to call the loan in for prepayment. Such events can range from the Channel Tunnel boring failing to reach mile 12.75 on a specified date, to mailing an annual report three days late to the lending bank.

Evergreen   A contract that rolls over after each agreed (short term) period until cancelled by one party.

Evergreen facility   A facility that automatically renews itself unless the borrower or lender gives notice to cancel.

Execute   Formal signing of documentation. Implement an action required under the documentation.

Expropriation   The state has taken over a company or project, implying compensation will be paid. Nationalization. Creeping expropriation occurs when a government squeezes a project by taxes, regulation, access, or changes in law.

Factoring   Selling of invoices to raise cash. Debts of various kinds are put together and sold to banks or corporate treasurers. A term used in international trade.

Fee   A fixed amount or a percentage of an underwriting or principal.

Final take   The final participation.

Finance lease   The lessor receives lease payments to cover its ownership costs. The lessee is responsible for maintenance, insurance and taxes. Some finance leases are conditional sales or hire purchase agreements.

Financial close   When the documentation has been executed and conditions precedent have been satisfied or waived. Drawdowns are now permissible.

Financial year end   The close of the year accounts (FYE).

Financing agreements   The documents which provide the project financing and sponsor support for the project as defined in the project contracts.

Fiscal year end   The end of the tax year as defined by the tax authorities.

Fixed cost   Operating cost which does not vary per unit of output.

Fixed rate   Interest rate that is fixed for a defined period.

Float   See IPO.

Floating rate   Interest rate that is reset periodically, usually every couple of months or sometimes daily.

Floor   A level which an interest rate or currency is structured not to go below.

Force majeure   Events outside the control of the parties. These events are acts of man, nature, governments/regulators, or impersonal events. Contract performance is forgiven or extended by the period of force majeure.

Forward contract   Forwards. An agreement to exchange currency or interest obligations in the future. For tradable commodities or securities, an agreement to buy or sell at a future date.

FRNs   Floating rate notes where the interest is reset by a panel or by reference to a market Floating Rate.

FRS/SSAP   Financial Reporting Standard/Statement of Standard Accounting Practices. A set of standardized guidelines and procedures which have become mandatory for directors in the UK for all company accounts.

Full recourse   No matter what risk event occurs, the borrower or its guarantors guarantee to repay the debt. By definition, this is not a project financing unless the borrower's sole asset is the project.

Funding risk   The impact on project cash flow from higher funding costs or lack of availability of funds. Interest Risk.

Futures   Agreements to purchase a commodity or financial instrument at a price agreed today. These are usually tradable on exchanges or computer trading screens.

Futures   These are formal agreements to purchase a given item in the future at a price agreed today. The purpose is to hedge against price changes. The practice began in Chicago in the 19th century and centred around the agricultural market, but records show that it was common in Holland and Japan in the 16th century.

Futures market   A market where forward contracts can be traded before their maturity.

FX   Foreign exchange; the conversion of one currency into another.

FX rate   Foreign exchange rate; one currency unit expressed in terms of another.

FX risk   The effect on project cash flow or debt service from a movement in the FX rate for revenue, costs, or debt service.

Gearing   This is a ratio that sums up the financial standing of a company. It is obtained by dividing the total interest-bearing debt by the shareholders' funds. The higher the number, the greater the risk. A company that has a large proportion of its permanent capital from debt is referred to as being highly geared.

General partner   The partner with unlimited liability.

Goodwill   The amount paid in excess of book value on the balance sheet, usually for intangible assets such as trademarks or licences.

Grace   After a default, days of grace may be stated within which the cure is effected. A period when interest or principal is not yet payable, usually a period after start-up/commissioning/completion in a project financing.

Guarantee   Usually an undertaking by a third party to assume the debts of the borrower in the event of default. A common situation with parent/affiliate lending arrangements. Guarantees can and do expire, and the analyst should ensure in the credit review that they are either still valid, or have been renewed.

Guarantor A party who will guarantee repayment or performance of a covenant.

Hedge To take a forward contract or option to effect an anticipated change in a currency, commodity, interest rate, or security, so that gains or losses are offset.

Hell-or-high-water An absolute commitment, with no contractual defence.

Hermes The trade finance agency for Germany.

Hire purchase The user of the asset is entitled to purchase the asset according to a pre-agreed method. The user may be the owner for tax purposes.

Hurdle rate A minimum IRR.

IDC Interest during construction. It usually equals capitalized interest.

IFC International Finance Corporation, the private enterprise arm of the World Bank.

Illiquid Not easily traded or not readily converted to cash.

Incipient default Potential default.

Income Operating cash flows less overheads and depreciation, either before tax (BT) or after tax (AT). Earnings.

Inconvertibility Where a local currency cannot be exchanged for another currency. Often includes transfer risk.

Indemnity A legal obligation to cover a liability, however arising.

Indexed rate An interest rate linked to an index, usually the CPI.

Information memorandum A document detailing the project and project financing, usually in connection with a syndication.

Infrastructure risk The impact on project cash flows from infrastructure problems. Sometimes labelled transportation risk.

Institutions Insurance companies, pension funds, trusts, foundations, mutual funds, funds managers, bank investment departments.

Instrument A financial tool. Sometimes a discrete type of funding or a security.

Intangible assets Good will, patents and trademark valuation, deferred charges, and share/bond premiums.

Interest Rate The percentage payable to the lender calculated at an annual rate on the principal. May be all-in.

Interest risk The impact on project cash flow from higher interest costs or lack of availability of funds. Funding risk.

Intermediary   An entity standing between parties to funding or a swap. An intermediary may be at risk.

Inverse order   Applied to the periodic repayment schedule and means from the end, expected maturity. 'Current order' means the next periodic principal repayment.

Investment bank   The US term for a merchant bank.

Investment grade   For a rating, the rating level above which institutional investors have been authorized to invest.

Investor/creditor community   Entities which provide funds to companies. Investors buy shares in the company (equity), while creditors lend money to companies (debt).

IPO   An initial public offering of shares. A float.

IPP   Independent power plant; an example of a BOO development.

IRR   The discount rate to make the NPV zero. Multiple IRRs occur mathematically if the periodic cash flows change sign more than once.

Islamic loan   Interest cannot be charged. Rather the loan is structured using discounts, sale/lease, profit participation, or repurchase agreements.

Joint venture   JV. The legal means of dividing the project's equity either by shareholdings in a company (incorporated JV) or by way of a contract (unincorporated JV).

Junk   A high-yield bond of speculative grade.

L/C   Letter of credit, a guarantee to pay limited to an amount and time triggered by defined events or exchange of agreed documents. Used for credit enhancement.

Latent default   A potential default that may have always been present but unidentified.

Lawsuit   In financial terms, this is a contingent liability, e.g. an item that does not appear on the balance sheet but can have a financial impact on the company. Lawsuits should be explained in the notes to the financial statements.

LDs   Liquidated damages. The amount payable for delays and substandard performance under a construction, equipment supply, or O&M contract.

Lead arranger   The senior tier of arranger.

Lead bank   A senior bank involved in the negotiations for a project financing. Subordinate to an arranger. Lead manager.

Lead manager   Senior tier of lender in a loan syndication.

League tables   A ranking of lenders and advisers according to the underwriting, final take or number of project finance loans or advisory mandates.

Lease   The owner of an asset (lessor) agrees to receive lease payments/rentals from the user (lessee), usually at a fixed rental level. The lessor/owner takes the benefit of depreciation as a tax deduction. Its primary security is the asset.

Lease rate   The equivalent interest rate calculated from a stream of lease payments.

Lease term   The life of a lease including any renewal options.

Legal risk   A risk that a defect in the documentation will affect cash flow or debt service.

Lending risk   The risk the bank is getting into by putting the loan into place. Often more narrowly defined as risk arising from inadequate or faulty loan documentation.

Lessee   The user who pays lease rentals to the owner/lessor.

Lessor   The owner of a leased asset.

Leverage   The American term for gearing. In the UK this is the same as gearing, with the addition of non-interest bearing external debt.

Leveraged lease   A lessor borrows to finance a leased asset. Recourse may be limited to the lease rentals or the asset.

Liability   The obligation to repay a defined amount or to perform a service.

LIBOR   London Interbank Offered Rate, often quoted as a 1,3,6-month rate for US$.

Lien   A legal security interest in an asset.

Limited recourse   Under certain conditions (legal or financial), there is access to the sponsor(s)' credit or other legal security for repayment (besides the project's cash flows). There is usually recourse in the event of fraud or misrepresentation/non-disclosure. Thus non-recourse is better described as 'limited recourse'.

Liquid   Easily traded or converted to cash.

Liquidation   Selling off the company's assets to satisfy creditors during a winding up. The main risk in a liquidation is asset shrinkage: whether the assets being liquidated can fetch a market value sufficient to satisfy all the creditors.

Liquidity   The ability to convert asset into cash. A measure of how easily assets can be converted into cash.

Loan agreement   Every loan should have one. These define the rules and obligations binding on the lenders, borrowers guarantors and related parties.

Loan officers   The persons who look after client relations and new business opportunities. The analyst's work is to evaluate objectively the companies and businesses loan officers are proposing to lend to, and submit their evaluations in the credit review process.

Loans, short term   Loans under one year's duration.

Loans, term   Loans of between 2 and 7 years' duration.

Long term   Three years or more. In accounting: more than 1 year.

Loss payee   A party to whom an insurance loss payment or settlement may be paid directly.

LP   Limited partner who is not liable for the debts of the partnership beyond the funds contributed.

Make-up   Where a cash flow or capital item is deficient, the amount of such deficiency, e.g. an interest make-up relates to the interest amount above a ceiling percentage.

Manager   A medium-level participant established according to final take.

Mandate   The formal appointment to advise on or arrange a project financing.

Margin   The amount expressed in % per annum above the interest rate basis or cost of funds. For hedging and futures contracts, the cash collateral deposited with a trader or exchange as insurance against default.

Market risk   Changes to the amounts sold or the price received which impacts on gross revenue. Sometimes called sales risk.

Maturity   The final date a project finance loan is repayable. The end of the term.

Maturity schedules   The repayment dates on the loan. A good set of company financial statements will break out all the various debt which it has, the interest rates and periods of repayment. The analyst should pay particular attention to the impact of bullet repayments on future cash flow.

Medium term   Two to six years.

Merchant bank A bank which, besides lending and deposit taking (usually not from the public), engages in trading, advisory services and as an underwriter and funds manager of securities.

MIGA Multilateral Investment Guaranty Agency, the PRI arm of the World Bank.

MILA Multilateral agency such as IFC, ADB.

MITI Ministry of International Trade and Industry of Japan.

Monetization Securitization of the gross revenues of a contract.

Monte Carlo Simulations using random numbers.

Negative pledge The borrower agrees not to pledge any of its assets as security and/or not to incur further indebtedness.

Negotiable A financial instrument can be bought or sold by another investor, privately or via a stock exchange/computer trading.

Non-recourse The financiers rely on the project's cash flows and collateral security over the project as the only means to repay debt service. This usually occurs after completion.

NPV The periodic net cash flows are each discounted by the discount rate to a present date and the appropriate cash outflows/investment for construction or acquisition are deducted from the total.

O&M Operations and maintenance.

Off-take(r) The purchase(r) of the project's output.

Operating cash flow Project revenues less (cash) Opex.

Operating risk Cost, technology and management components which impact Opex and project output/throughput. Costs includes inflation.

Opex Operating expenses, always expressed as cash. Therefore, depletion and depreciation are excluded.

Option A contract in which the writer of the option grants the buyer of the option the right, but not the obligation, to purchase from or sell to the writer something at a specified price within a specified period of time (or a specified date).

Oversubscription Underwriting commitments from a syndication exceed the amount sought by the amount of oversubscription.

Overrun The amount of Capex or funding above the original estimate to complete the project.

p. a. per annum, yearly.

Pari passu   Equal ranking of security pro-rata to the amount owed.

Participant   A party to a funding. It usually refers to the lowest rank/ smallest level of funding. Alternatively, it is one of the parties to the project financing/or the project documents.

Participant risk   The credit of the participants and the risk of non-performance under the project contracts or financing agreements.

Participation   The amount of loan/bond issue taken directly or from another direct lender/underwriter.

Partnership   The partners agree to a proportional share of profits and losses and thus have the same tax treatment.

Payback   The period in years to recover the investment or loan. It may be calculated on a discounted, non-discounted, leveraged, or unleveraged basis.

Payment   The amount is that required to repay a loan with interest and fees.

Performance bond   A bond of 5–10% of a contract payable if a project is not completed as specified. Usually part of a construction contract or supply agreement.

Physical completion   The project is physically functioning, but not yet (fully) generating cash flow.

Placement   Securities are placed with a small group of Investors.

Point   One percentage point on a note or bond.

Political risk   Eight risks usually comprising currency inconvertibility, expropriation, war and insurrection, terrorism, environmental activities, landowner actions, non-government activists, legal, and bureaucratic/ approvals. The first three are insurable. It overlaps with the political component of force majeure risk.

Potential default   A condition where a default would occur in time or where a notice or default event has not yet been formalized.

PPA   Power purchase agreement, a long term power supply contract.

Premium   The cost of an insurance policy. The price of an option. An extra margin payable with prepayment of principal.

Prepayment   Repayment of greater than the scheduled amount. If forced, it is referred to as a mandatory prepayment.

PRI   Political risk insurance.

Prime rate   A (US) bank interest rate charged to prime customers for loans (in excess of $100 000).

Principal   The quantity of the outstanding project financing due to be paid. Generic: a principal is a party bearing an obligation or responsibility directly (as distinct from an agent).

Private placement   The placement of debt or equity investment is not publicized and may not be tradable.

Pro rata   Shared or divided according to a ratio or in proportion to their participations.

Production   A defined portion of the proceeds of production up to a dollar amount.

Production loan   A project financing where the repayment is linked to the production, often on a $/unit basis.

Proforma   A financial projection based on assumptions.

Project   The asset constructed with or owned via a project financing which is expected to produce cash flow at a debt service cover ratio sufficient to repay the project financing.

Project contracts   The suite of agreements underlying the project.

Project financing   A loan structure which relies for its repayment primarily on the project's cash flow with the project's assets, rights and interests held as secondary security or collateral.

Prospectus   A formally approved document describing the business and affairs of the issuer and the terms and conditions of the security. An offering circular in the USA, filed with the SEC, e.g. for an IPO or a Rule 144a Bond Issue.

Purchasing power parity   A view that differential escalation rates (in different countries) determine the systematic change in FX rates.

Put   An option to sell (back) a security or commodity at a set price at a given.

PV   Present value where a stream of cash flows or accounting flows are discounted to the present at a discount rate.

Rating   The ranking, usually grades of A to E, of the creditworthiness/ability to repay. The ranking of bonds is related to its estimated percentage default rate. Countries are similarly ranked and may include an estimation of political risk.

Ratio analysis   The technique of analysing company performance by calculating financial ratios for historical and comparative purposes.

Receiver   A person/entity appointed under the legal security documents to administer the security on behalf of the project financiers.

Recourse In the event that the project (and its associated escrows, sinking funds, or cash reserves/standby facilities) cannot service the financing or completion cannot be achieved, then the financiers have recourse to either cash from other sponsor/corporate sources or other non-project security.

Refinancing Repaying existing debt and entering into a new loan, typically to meet some corporate objective such as the lengthening of maturity or lowering the interest rate.

Regulatory actions Legal requirements on a company; for example, a government passes a law forcing a chemical companies to process carcinogenic waste instead of dumping it. Regulatory actions can adversely impact a company's profitability and viability.

Representations A series of statements about a project, a sponsor, or the obligations under the project contracts or the financing agreements.

Reserve account A separate amount of cash or L/C to service a payment requirement such as debt service or maintenance.

Residual The assumed value of an asset at the end of a loan, lease, or proforma cash flow. It is sometimes insured.

Residual cover The cash flow remaining after a project financing has been repaid expressed as a percentage of the original loan.

Residual cushion The amount of net cash flow from the project after the project financing has been repaid. If it is expressed as a percentage of the original loan amount, it is the 'residual cover'.

Retention An amount held back from construction contract payments to ensure the contractor completes the construction before the retention (5–15% of the contract price) is returned to the contractor.

Return on assets (ROA) Net profits after taxed divided by assets. This ratio helps a firm determine how effectively it generates profits from available assets.

Return on equity (ROE) Net profits after taxes divided by stockholders' equity.

Revenues Sales or royalty proceeds. Quantity times price realized.

Risk The event which can change the expected cash flow forecast for the project financing. 'At risk' means the cash or loan. For insurance, it means the total amount or type of event insured.

ROCE Return on capital employed.

Royalty   A share of revenue or cash flow to the government or grantor of the concession or licence.

Rule 144a   Under US SEC regulations, a Rule 144a security (usually bonds but can be equity/shares) can be placed with professional investors who are prequalified/registered and take minimum US$100 000 amounts. Less strict document/disclosure/due diligence is permitted than a full prospectus.

SACE   The Italian ECA.

Sales completion   The project has reached physical completion and has delivered product or generated revenues in satisfaction of a sales completion test.

Salvage value   The estimated selling price of an asset once it has been fully depreciated.

SEC   Securities & Exchange Commission, which regulates disclosure and practices for companies and public issues of debt and equity in the USA.

Securitization   Bundling up a stream of receivables (e.g. mortgage payments or credit card payments) to sell on the capital markets as an investment, with future payments comprising the 'return on investment'.

Security   A legal right of access to value through mortgages, contracts, cash accounts, guarantees, insurances, pledges, or cash flow including licences, concessions and other Assets. A negotiable certificate evidencing a debt or equity obligation/shareholding.

Security   The assets or guarantees you claim when the loan is in default. Forms of security can vary from high grade government bonds to partially completed stock, and are defined in the loan agreement.

Security agreement   An agreement in which title to property is held as collateral under a financing agreement, usually by a trustee.

Senior   Ranking for repayment, security, or action. Most project financings are senior debt obligations with first, senior security.

Sensitivity   A change to a cash flow input to determine the change to DSCR.

Setoff   Money held on behalf of a borrower may be applied to repay the loan. It usually implies without the permission of the borrower.

Shareholders' equity   Net worth. Book value of total assets less total liabilities.

Short term   Up to 12 months.

Sinking fund   A regular payment is set aside in anticipation of a future payment.

SOE   State-owned enterprise.

Sovereign risk   The government's part of political risk.

Sponsor   A party wishing to develop a project. A developer. A party providing financial support.

Spreadsheet   The analyst's main tool in unscrambling a typical set of company accounts.

Steam turbine   Electricity generation from steam pressure.

Structure   How a project financing is drawn down, repaid and collateralized secured.

Subordinated   The subordinated party accepts a lower priority of repayment and/or security than senior debt.

Sunk costs   Capital already spent.

Supplier credit   The supplier of goods or services agrees to deferred repayment terms.

Supply risk   The raw materials or input to a project change from those assumed/projected. For a resources production project, this is called reserves risk.

Swap   An exchange of the basis of obligations to repay principal, interest, or currency. For interest-rate swaps (floating to fixed), the underlying principal may not be exchanged.

Sweep   All available cash flow is used for debt service.

Syndication   The selling of a project finance to a group of prospective participants, the syndicate.

Tail   The remaining reserves after the project financing has been repaid. Sometimes means the residual.

Take-and-pay   If the project's output is deliverable and can be taken, it will be paid for.

Take-or-pay   In the event the project's output is not taken, payment must be made whether or not the output is deliverable.

Takeout   A financing to refinance or take out another, e.g. construction, loan.

Tenor   The number of years a loan is outstanding. The term.

Term   The loan life or tenor; the period to a loan's maturity. Generic: a condition attached.

Throughput   A throughput agreement is a hell-or-high-water contract to put and pay for material through a facility. Force majeure gives no relief.

TNW Total net worth.

Tolling A contract to process or convert a raw material into a saleable or finished product. The tolling contract does not require the purchase of the raw material or the sale of the output.

Tombstone An advertisement listing the sponsor, amount funded, participants and key roles.

Tranche A separate portion of a project financing, perhaps with different financiers, margins, and term.

Transfer risk Currency cannot be sent out of the country, usually due to central bank restrictions or a national debt rescheduling.

Trustee An independent or nominated third party who administers corporate or financial arrangements.

Turnkey The construction of a project to meet a standard or the completion test where it is ready to produce cash flow. Turnkey contracts usually have LDs and retentions.

Underwriting The commitment to fund is not contingent on syndication.

Unsecured The financier has no security, merely the obligation/ undertaking to repay.

Unwind To reverse a swap or hedge.

WACC Weighted average cost of capital calculated from the returns on interest rates payable on the different components of a company's or a project's deemed capital structure.

Withholding A tax on interest, royalty, or dividend payments, usually those paid overseas. It may be deducted at source.

Working capital Cash required to fund inventories and accounts receivable. Accounting definition is current assets less current liabilities. It is recovered entirely when the project ceases.

Workout The project financiers are responding to work out a potential problem or have arranged to take over the operation after a default to attempt to rehabilitate the cash flow generating capacity of the project.

World Bank An MILA based in Washington, DC. The International Bank for Reconstruction and Development. Usually involved in government-related deals.

Yield Usually expressed as a percentage, this represents the return earned from an investment.

Zero coupon No interest is paid. A bond or note is issued at a discount which is calculated to yield a compound interest equivalent return.

Suggested reading

Publications

Project Finance International: biweekly magazine published by Thomson Financial.

Infrastructure Journal: The on-line resource for infrastructure professionals.

PFI Intelligence Bulletin (SMI Publishing, UK): PFI Intelligence Bulletin is a newsletter covering PFI legislation, regulation, working procedures, and market potential including database of PFI projects (800 in total) within the UK and beyond.

Project Finance Magazine: a monthly trade journal published by Euromoney Publications PLC.

Project Finance Monthly: a monthly trade journal published by Infocast.

Books

Beenhakker, H.L. (1997) *Risk Management in Project Finance and Implementation*. Westport, CT: Quorum Books.

Benoit, P. (1996) *Project Finance at the World Bank: An Overview of Policies and Instruments*, (World Bank Technical Paper Number 312). Washington DC: The World Bank.

Esty, Benjamin, C. (2004) *Modern Project Finance: A Casebook*. New York, NY: John Wiley & Sons.

Euromoney Institutional Investor (2005) *Project Finance Yearbook 2004/2005*.

Fitzgerald, P.F., and Machlin, B.N. (2001) *Project Financing: Building Infrastructure Projects in Developing Markets (2001)*. New York, NY: Practising Law Institute.

Frame, J. Davidson (2003) *Project Finance: Tools and Techniques.* Arlington, VA: University of Management and Technology (UMT) Press.

Fight, A. (2006) *Cash Flow Forecasting*. Oxford: Elsevier Butterworth-Heinemann.

Fight, A. (2000) *The Ratings Game*. Wiley & Sons.

International Finance Corporation (1999) *Project Finance in Developing Countries, (Lessons of Experience Number 7)*. Washington DC: World Bank.

International Finance Corporation (2002) *The Environmental and Social Challenges of Private Sector Projects: IFC's Experience, (Lessons of Experience Number 8)*. Washington DC: World Bank.

International Finance Corporation (1999) *The Private Sector Financing Activities of International Financial Institutions 1991–1997*. Washington DC.

Lang, L.H.P. (1998) *Project Finance in Asia (Advances in Finance, Investment, and Banking, V. 6)*. Elsevier Science Ltd (North-Holland).

Miller, J.B. (2000) *Principles of Public and Private Infrastructure Delivery*. Boston, MA: Kluwer Academic Publishers and the American Infrastructure Consortium.

Razavi, H. (1996) *Financing Energy Projects in Emerging Economies*. Tulsa, OK: PennWell.

Scheinkestel, N.L. (1997) *Rethinking Project Finance: Allocating and Mitigating Risk in Australasian Projects*. Hong Kong: Asia Law & Practice Publishing Ltd.

Squire, L. and van der Tak, H.G. (1975) *Economic Analysis of Projects*. Baltimore, MD: Johns Hopkins University Press.

The World Bank and International Finance Corporation (1996) *Financing Private Infrastructure*. Washington DC.

Index

Abandonment, 134
Account bank, 14
Additional indebtedness, 120
Advance payment guarantees, 114
Advanced loss of revenue insurance, 78
Advisers, 87
African Development Bank, 28
American International Underwriters, 22
Anderson, Geoff, 140
Applicable laws and jurisdiction, 59
Arab Fund for Economic and Social Development, 28
Arranger, 13–14
Asian Development Bank, 28–9
Authority letter, 86

Bankruptcy, 134
Banks *see individual types*
Bid (tender) bonds, 80, 114
Bonds, 40–1, 80
  bid (tender), 80, 114
  contractors, 114–15
  maintenance, 114–15
  payment, 80

performance, 80, 114
  retention money, 80
Borrower, 12, 86
Breach of credit support, 135
Bretton Woods Conference, 25
Building materials, 53
Business risk, 123

Capital costs, 94–5
Capital expenditure, 131
Capitalization, 111
Cash deficiency agreement, 116
Cash deficiency guarantee, 72
Cash flow, 95–7
Cash flow forecasts, 1
Citicorp International Trade Indemnity, Inc., 22
Claw-back guarantee, 72
Collateral, 6, 86, 109
Commercial banks, 9
Commercial insurance, 22, 24
Commitment, 87
Compagnie Française d'Assurances Commerciale Exterieure, 21–2, 23
Companies Act (1985), 84
Compensation account, 132–3

Competitive market exposure,
    109–10
Completion delays, 53
Completion guarantee, 64, 72
Completion risks, 53
Completion test, 64–5
Concession agreements, 112–13
Concessions, 112
Conditions precedent, 119, 135–6
Construction agreements, 113–14
Construction companies, 18, 30–1
    as finance sources, 42–3
Construction and development
    phase, 11
Construction lenders, risk
    analysis, 46
Construction phase guarantees, 71
Construction reports, 136
Consultants, 87
Consultant's report, 136
Contingent guarantees, 73
Contractor risk, 47, 53
Contractor's all risks insurance, 77–8
Contractors bonds, 114–15
Contracts, 90
Contractual framework, 112–38
    construction agreements, 113–14
    contractors bonds, 114–15
    management agreements,
        116–17
    operating and maintenance
        agreements, 115–16
    pre-development agreements,
        112–13
    project loan/credit agreements,
        118–37
    representations and warranties,
        117–18
    security agreements, 137–8
    sponsor support agreements, 116
Control accounts, 132–3
Conversion, 54

Corporate substance, 52
Cost overruns, 53, 64, 87, 131
Counterparty exposure, 110
Counterparty risk, 55–6
Country risk, 57–9, 94, 156–65
Covenants, 121–7
    breach of, 133
    drawbacks to, 124–5
    events of default, 126–7
    functions of, 124
    guidelines, 125
    project financing, 127–31
    types of, 126
Cover ratios, 131–2
Coverage ratios, 100–1
Credit agency rating scales, 153–5
Credit agreements, 119–20
Credit enhancement, 87
Credit risk appraisal, 108–11
    financial strength, 110–11
    post-construction, 108–10
    pre-construction, 108

Debt, 86
Debt amortization, 87, 97
Debt ratios, 100
Debt service ratio, 104
Debt service reserve account, 133
Depreciation, 94–5
Development banks, 24–30
Developmental loan, 33
Direct lending, 40
Disbursement account, 132
Disclaimer, 86
Discounted cash flow model, 94
Distribution of dividends, 120–1
Dividend decisions, 122–3
Documentation, 129
    security, 130, 135, 137
Drawdown cover ratio, 132
Drawdowns, 87, 119
Due diligence, 51

Economic information, 90
Economic risks, 156–62
Eksportkreditraadet (Denmark), 23
Energy sector, 2
Enforceability of contracts, 60
Engineering and construction phase
    risks, 51–3
Entity risks, 45–50
    construction lender, 46
    contractor, 47
    equity investor, 49
    host government, 48–9
    multilateral and bilateral
        agencies, 49–50
    off-taker/purchaser, 48
    operator, 47–8
    other governments, 49
    permanent lender, 46–7
    sponsor, 45–6
    supplier, 48
Environmental compliance, 129
Environmental legislation, 93
Environmental review, 136
Environmental risk, 60–1
EPC contract, 10, 18
Equity, 32–3, 86
Equity contributions, 109
Equity investors, 15–18
    risk analysis, 49
European Bank for Reconstruction
    and Development, 24–5, 29
European Investment Bank, 29
European Union, 29
Evaluation of project, 81–111
    credit risk appraisal, 108–11
    information memoranda, 83–107
    offering memorandum, 81–3
Events of default, 120, 126–7, 133–5
Exchange rate fluctuations, 78
Export credit agencies, 19–24, 40
Export Credit Insurance Company
    (Spain), 24

Export Credits Guarantee
    Department, 20–1, 24
Export Development Corporation of
    Canada, 22, 23
Export Finance and Insurance
    Corporation (Australia), 23
Export financing, 78
Export-Import Bank of Japan, 20, 23
Export-Import Bank of Korea, 23
Expropriation, 134

Facility agent, 14
Facility site, 53
Feasibility studies, 50–1
Fees, 6–7, 87
Final acceptance date, 134
Financial adviser, 12–13
Financial covenants, 126
Financial flexibility, 111
Financial intermediary loans, 40
Financial ratio analysis, 97–101
Financial reporting, 130
Financial risks, 56–7, 110
    mitigation and management, 68
Financial Services Act (1986), 84, 85
Financial tests, 130
Financing decisions, 122
Financing sources, 32–44
Financing terms, 5
Finnish Export Credit Limited, 23
Fixed costs, 95
Fixed price lump sum contract, 64
Force majeure, 62
Foreign exchange risk, 56, 93–4
Forward contracts, 68
Futures contracts, 68

Garanti instituttet for Eksportkreditt
    (Norway), 23
Global syndicated loans, 38, 39
Government approvals, 134
Government assurances, 73

Grace periods, 121
Guarantee Program, 39–40
Guarantees, 71–3

Highways, 3
Hong Kong Interbank Offered Rate, 87
Host governments, 30, 90–1
  risk analysis, 48–9
  as sources of finance, 43–4
Housing development cash flow
  sensitivity analysis, 104–7

Illegality clause, 119
Implied guarantees, 72
Indebtedness, 129
Independent engineers, 92
Indirect guarantees, 72
Inflation risk, 57, 111
Information memoranda, 87–107
  legislation applying to, 83–7
Institutional lenders, 42
Instituto Centrale per il Credito a
  Medio Termine (Italy), 23
Insurance, 7, 77–80, 121, 129
  commercial, 22, 24
  performance and payment bonds,
   80
  problem areas, 79–80
  reinsurance, 80
  role of, 77
  scope of cover, 79
  types of, 77–8
Insurance bank, 14
Insurers, 31–2
Inter-American Development
  Bank, 30
Intercompany loans, restrictions
  on, 121
Intercreditor agreement, 136–7
Interest clause, 119
Interest rate, 6–7, 87
Interest rate equalization, 40

Interest rate risk, 56–7, 111
International Finance Corporation,
  27
Investment appraisal, 94
Investment decisions, 123
Investment funds, 42
Islamic Development Bank, 30

Joint venture agreements, 70, 113
Judgments, 134

Kreditanstalt für Wiederaufbau
  (Germany), 23

Lawyers, 15, 87
Leasing companies, 31, 42
Legal risks, 59–60
Lender liability risk, 62–4
Lenders, 13–14
  reporting requirements, 7
  risk, 6
  supervision required by, 7
Letters of comfort, 72, 116
Leveraged debt, 5
Limited guarantees, 71
Limited recourse project finance, 4
Limited rights to appeal, 59
Liquidated damages, 65
Liquidity ratios, 98–100
Liquidity risk, 57, 111
Lloyd's of London, 22
Loan life cover ratio, 131–2
Loan Program, 39
Loans *see various types*
London Interbank Offered Rate, 87
Long term supply contracts, 65

Maintenance agreement, 116
Maintenance bonds, 114–15
Maintenance reserve account, 133
Management agreements, 116–17
Managers, 14

Margin protection clauses, 119
Marine advanced loss of revenue
    insurance, 78
Marine cargo insurance, 78
Market, 91–2
Mezzanine financing, 33–4
Milestone dates, 130
Mining industry, 3
Ministry of Economy Trade and
    Industry (Japan), 20
Moody's issuer rating symbols, 153
Multilateral agencies, 24–30
    risk analysis, 49–50
Multilateral Investment Guarantee
    Agency, 27–8

Negative pledge, 75, 120
Net present value, 94, 131–2
Non-financial covenants, 126
Non-recourse project financing,
    3–4
Nordic Development Fund, 30
Nordic Investment Bank, 30
Norquist, Grover, 2, 140
Notice of events, 128
NPV *see* net present value

O&M contract, 10
Obligations, payment of, 134–5
Oesterreichische Kontrollbank AG, 23
Off balance sheet debt, 4–5
Off-take agreements, 10
Off-take contracts, 109
Off-take/sales risk, 48, 55
Offering memorandum, 81–3
Office National du Decroire
    (Belgium), 23
Oil industry, 2
OPEC Fund for International
    Development, 30
Operating budget, 130
Operating costs, 95

Operating and maintenance
    agreements, 115–16
Operating/performance risk, 54–5
Operation phase, 11
Operational risks, 54–6
    mitigation and management, 65–7
Operator's all risks insurance, 78
Operator's loss of revenue coverage,
    78
Operators risk analysis, 47–8
Options, 68
Organization for Economic
    Co-operation and Development,
    22
Overseas Private Investment
    Corporation (USA), 24
Ownership, 134

Partnership agreements, 113
Payment bonds, 80
Performance bonds, 80, 114
Permanent lenders, risk analysis,
    46–7
Permits and licensing, 59, 61, 93,
    112, 135
Political risk, 57–9, 156
    mitigation and management,
    68–70
Political risk insurance, 69, 70
Porter's Risk Assessment Matrix, 91
Pre-completion risk, 52
Pre-development agreements, 112–13
Private Finance Initiative, 145–50
Private market insurance, 69
Privatization, 139–45
Proceeds account, 132
Product pricing, 57
Profitability, 93
Progress reports, 127–8
Project company, 11–12
Project finance
    advantages of, 4–6

Project finance (*contd*)
  definition, 1–2
  disadvantages of, 6–7
  misconceptions, 7–8
  parties to, 11–32
  reasons for using, 3–8
  uses of, 2–3
Project finance tables, 145, 146–9
Project finance transactions, 8–11
Project financing covenants, 127–31
Project life cover ratio, 131
Project loan/credit agreements,
    118–37
  basic terms, 119–20
  conditions precedent to closing,
    135–6
  control accounts, 132–3
  covenants, 121–7
  events of default, 133–5
  intercreditor agreement, 136–7
  NPVs and cover ratios, 131–2
  project finance credit agreements,
    120–1
  project financing covenants,
    127–31
Project overview, 86
Project participants, 89
Project phases, 11
Project risks, 94
Public opposition, 61
Purchasers, 31

Quasi-equity, 33–4

Raw materials
  access to, 92
  risk, 55
Real estate, 135
Refinancing risk, 61
Regional development banks, 28–30
Regulatory agencies, 18–19
Regulatory risks, 61

Reinsurance, 80
Related facilities, 53
Repayment clause, 119
Repayment cover ratio, 132
Representation, 117–18, 119
  breach of, 133–4
Reserve accounts, 121
Restrictive covenants, avoidance of, 5
Retention guarantees, 114
Retention money bonds, 80
Risk, 45–80, 152
  entity risks, 45–50
  insurance, 77–80
  mitigation and management,
    64–73
  security, 73–7
  transaction risks, 50–64
Risk allocation, complexity of, 6
Risk assessment, transaction risks,
    50–1
Risk diversification, 5
Risk periods, 51–6
  engineering and construction
    phase risks, 51–3
  operational risks, 54–6
  start-up risks, 54
Risk sharing, 5–6

Sales/off-take agreements, 115
Schedule, 90
Secured loans, 35
Security, 59, 73–7
  formalities, 77
  negative pledge, 75
  reasons for, 74
  security trusts, 75–6
  specific tangible assets, 74–5
Security agreements, 137–8
Security documents, 130, 135, 137
Security trustee, 14
Security trusts, 75–6
Senior debt, 34–5

Sensitivity analysis, 101–4
  housing development cash flow,
    104–7
Shareholder agreements, 113
Site and permitting risks, 53
Sovereign guarantees, 73
Special purpose vehicles, 5, 10
Specific tangible assets, 74–5, 137–8
Sponsor, 12, 43, 86, 88, 108
Sponsor guarantees, 87
Sponsor risk, 45–6, 52
Sponsor support agreements, 116
Standard & Poor's long term debt
    ratings, 154
Standard & Poor's short term
    commercial paper debt ratings,
    155
Standard & Poor's sovereign rating
    profile, 162–5
Start-up risks, 54
Structural risk, 60
Subordinated loans, 33–4
Supplier financing, 43
Suppliers, 31
  risk analysis, 48
Supply contract, 10
Supply risk, 55
Supply-or-pay agreements, 115
Swaps, 68
Swedish International Development
    Authority, 24
Syndicated lending, 1
Syndicated loans, 36–8
Syndicates, 13

Take-and-pay contract, 66–7, 115
Take-or-pay contracts, 65–6, 115
Tax breaks, 5
Technical adviser, 15

Technical information, 89–90
Technical/engineering bank, 14
Technology/obsolescence risk, 56
Telecommunications, 3
Third party liability, 78
Throughput agreements, 67, 115–16
Transaction risks, 50–64
  country/political risks, 57–9
  environmental, regulatory and
    approval risks, 60–1
  financial risks, 56–7
  force majeure, 62
  legal risks, 59–60
  lender liability risk, 62–4
  preliminary risk assessment, 50–1
  refinancing risk, 61
  risk periods, 51–6
Trustee accounts, 131
Turnkey contract, 18, 64

Under investment, 123
Undertakings, 120
Unistat Assurance, 22
United States Export–Import Bank,
    19–20, 24
Unlimited guarantees, 72
Unsecured loans, 34–5

Variable costs, 95
Vendor financing of equipment, 42

Warranties, 78, 117–18, 119
  breach of, 133–4
Working capital agreement, 116
World Bank, 25–7
  country categories, 166–74
  group financing sources, 38–40
  Partial Risk Guarantee
    Program, 40

Printed and bound by CPI Group (UK) Ltd, Croydon, CR0 4YY

08/05/2025

01864777-0002